Tony Allen

A SUMMER
IN THE PARK

Tony Allen

A SUMMER
IN THE PARK

A journal written from diary notes
June 4th 2000 to October 16th 2000

FREEDOM PRESS
LONDON

Published in 2004 by
Freedom Press
84B Whitechapel High Street
London E1 7QX

ISBN 1 904491 04 9

Front cover photograph by Ishmahil Blagrove
Back cover photograph by Hen Altof
Design and typesetting by Jayne Clementson

Printed in Great Britain by Aldgate Press
Units 5/6 Gunthorpe Workshops, Gunthorpe Street, London E1 7RQ

Many thanks to

Richard Baker, Tony Bennett, Ishmahil Blagrove, Helen Cherry, Farrell Cleary, Jayne Clementson, Grant Geary, Matt Harvey, Jimini Hignet, Roy Hutchins, Den Levett, John Miles, Rory Motion, Martin Peacock, Andy Porter, Vernon Trilby, James Waite, Philip Wolmuth, Andy West and Zac the Snap.

The author wishes it to be known that he gave up smoking both tobacco and cannabis in August 2002 and has been getting up before midday and feeling much healthier ever since.

The names of certain participants mentioned in this journal have been changed to avoid embarrassment.

CONTENTS

FOREWORD

To be honest I'm finding it very difficult to write this foreword to Tony Allen's A Summer In The Park. I now realise that to write a proper regular introduction your introducer has to fancy himself superior to the work he is introducing. Should the job be attempted from the position of humbled?

Honesty and clarity are two things which Tony's book has (in spades). So what, honestly, and as clearly as I can recall it, was my initial reaction to A Summer In The Park? It was this – Gosh, wow, fuck, phew, hooray. Would that in fact be my best offering for a foreword? i.e.

FOREWORD
Gosh! Wow!! Fuck!!! Phew! Hooray!!
Ken Campbell

When I got to the end of A Summer In The Park, I immediately read it again, this time underlining everything I particularly liked. I underlined the *whole thing*! There are repetitions in the book, and yes I underlined them – joyfully. These repetitions *sing*.

I attempted a list of the sorts and types of folk I thought would get off on this book as much as me: 'Orators, hecklers, comedians, wits, performance artists, cabaret artistes, actors, audiences, clowns, critics, journalists, novelists, anarchists, socialists, liberals, Tories, squatters, property owners (especially them with mortgages), landlords, anyone in rented accommodation, the homeless, anyone who works for a living, anyone who works for a living and wishes one didn't, anyone living. The un-dead.'

What is it then, this wonderful book? Well, in the summer of 2000 Tony Allen was the recipient of a modest Arts Council grant to be an Advocate Heckler at Hyde Park Speakers' Corner. This is the account of how he didn't do that. Instead he became a speaker.

What stuns is Tony's enthusiasm to pick himself and his art apart, to dwell (fully and healthily) on his many shortcomings and failures as an Hyde Park Orator, and in so doing he throws up more insights into the performer's art than any other book I know. (If you've got Keith Johnstone's *Impro*, this is the book to sit next to it on your shelf.)

I plead we get more summers, Tony. More summers! More summers!!

Ken Campbell
February 2004

INTRODUCTION

Speakers' Corner is situated at the North East tip of Hyde Park near Marble Arch. Because of its low status, peculiar social history and free admission, it resembles something that might have evolved from bare-knuckle boxing or cock fighting. The truth of course is even more macabre. Up until 1783 people gathered at the Tyburn Gallows – junction of Edgware Road and Oxford Street – to witness public executions and listen to the final words of condemned men. The right of public assembly inside the park was established as a result of riots in 1866 and ever since people have gathered here to talk, listen, chat, argue and speak their piece. The legacy is a unique culture of licence and familiarity which allows complete strangers to fall into conversations that might just as easily result in a profound communion as a heated slanging match. While not an exclusive male domain, over 90% of the speakers and regulars are men and the proportion of one-off visitors and tourists is still over 60% male. Public speaking, like stand-up comedy, is a predominantly male form – pushy, up-front and potentially penetrating. I am aware that this journal often appears to be documenting the goings-on at a bizarre down-market gentlemen's club.

Cynics and woollies

Among the many thousands who come and go each Sunday, hundreds are long-term denizens and of them over forty will be regular speakers. At any

Peter England, 1977

given time, at least a dozen of them can been seen and heard striving to engage the endlessly shifting population, with everything from calls to revolution to warnings of personal damnation. For as long as I can remember, grumpy cynics have dismissed Speakers' Corner as an over-policed, cheap tourist attraction, while woolly liberals celebrate a long-standing bastion of free speech. I'm local, I could argue that it's both, either or neither.

Old lag consensus

The current consensus among the old lags is that Speakers' Corner is dominated by a plethora of religious fanatics and has seen much better days – yesterday's speakers were far superior to the current crop, the hecklers were wittier, the crowds bigger and the characters more exotic. I can't be doing with this view of things, it's sentimental and ridiculously lop-sided; of course the sum total of all our yesterdays are going to be objectively more interesting than last Sunday, but the truth is that Speakers' Corner in the year 2000 is in pretty good shape. At the height of a summer's afternoon the crowds are as large as ever they were, there's always plenty of meetings on the go. There's enough eccentrics and crazies around to add a bit of local colour without scaring too many tourists, and the police, while still making mistakes exercising their unnecessary powers, intervene far less, make fewer arrests and generally have a much lower profile. Add to this, that arguably the three most interesting speakers – Heiko Khoo, Ishmahil Blagrove and Yusef – are all under forty and speak on very different platforms. Plus, in the light entertainment, romantic lead category, Martin Besserman is the best for generations.

My First Heckle

I can't even remember my first visit to Speakers' Corner. It was always there, part of the West London cultural landscape, a low dive of a place where they openly argued about royalty, religion and politics – taboo subjects in our house. But I can remember my first contribution – it was embarrassing. In the early sixties, as an impressionable teenager at the very

Funny walk Norman, 1979

beginning of my political education, I was stood alongside a working-class-hero style grey-haired communist, supporting him while he defended the Russian invasion of Hungary. "If communism's so good, why are people still leaving in their droves?" shouted a heckler. "Because they're fascists!" I piped up immediately. No one said anything, but it all went quiet for a second or two, while it registered. Then everyone, including the speaker, totally ignored me and what I'd said and carried on arguing. It was a very lonely and potent moment. I didn't go back for six months and when I did,

Andrew Ogilvy, 1979

I made damn sure I kept me mouth shut. But I'd learned one thing – what it felt like to die in public.

'The Speakers'

I lived in the suburbs in those days and was never what you'd call a regular. I can vaguely remember the well-known characters from that period: Axel the anarchist, a booming demagogue gesticulating from behind a high lectern; Van Dyne the tattooed man, who made bizarre noises and looked like a scary fairground freak; McGuiness, a down-at-heel Brendan Behan type, holding court half-pissed, leaning on the railings; Smithy the tramp, a furtive low-life joker who recited a lewd horse race commentary using names from the Profumo affair. I'm not even sure how much of this is actual and how much implanted due to a later reading of Heathcote Williams' book *The Speakers* (and then seeing the stage play).

Ogilvy

In the early seventies I joined a street theatre group and moved to Ladbroke Grove and my visits were more frequent. I became a squatting activist and called myself an anarchist and I'd adopted Heathcote Williams as my mentor. I went to the Corner with him just the once and surprisingly he was only interested in listening to one speaker – Andrew Ogilvy, the witty and articulate old Scot.

Ogilvy was an independent voice, too wise to ever join a party or subscribe to a creed; and while he was no leader of men, he was always surrounded by a group of loyal listeners who stayed with him for hours on end. They felt like a humanist congregation, which is roughly what they were; I can even recall seeing a collection being taken in his meeting.

Dramatic conflict – raw and obvious

It wasn't until I acquired a weekly Speakers' Corner habit in the late seventies that I started heckling with any success and fluency. But like most hecklers I harboured a serious fantasy to one day take the plunge and become a speaker.

At this time I was a member of an experimental busking troupe and developing my skills as a barker and MC, but nothing can prepare you for the Hyde Park speaking experience. The performance dynamics are unique. The close proximity of other meetings and the robust heckling tradition make Speakers' Corner unlike any other forum of public performance. Having an audience of easily distracted browsers harbouring hit and run snipers demands a house style of 'dramatic conflict' raw and obvious. A take-no-prisoners gladiatorial confrontation with the speaker as devil's advocate was, and remains, the preferred tried and tested format. Even the rough-house of street theatre was subtle by comparison.

What is intellectual property?

There is no copyright in a slanging match. Familiar old jokes and heckler put-downs can be heard from a range of different speakers in a variety of meetings; there are even quite complicated exchanges being routinely trotted out. In specific contexts a sort of public information banter has evolved. Particular hecklers confront particular speakers with identical arguments on a tiresomely regular basis. Each week Anarchists have to explain over and over again who will maintain the sewers after the revolution; Socialists reiterate endlessly how the Soviet Union was in fact state capitalism; and Born Again Christians spend their time explaining how and why newborn babies have sinned against God. The text varies little from one week, month or year to the next. New speakers – and new adversaries – emerge repeating the familiar unwritten scripts. This peculiar oral folk tradition stretches back across the decades, centuries, and beyond – even Christ's disciples must have been heckled with a version of: "If God is so all knowing and all understanding how come he sent a tosser like you to convert me?"

Upping the ante

Across a range of subjects, most of the basic arguments and formulas to attract and maintain a crowd already exist. Brief racist, sexist or homophobic statements, even if they are quickly recanted or made light of, can up the ante, trigger heckles and swell the audience. Expressions of religious fundamentalism or political extremism will also serve, just so long as the speaker is willing to argue his corner. Even a new speaker who has not emerged from the immediate gene pool will quickly adopt many of the local characteristics after a few hours of cross-pollination via the hecklers. It is only the originality of individual speakers and to a lesser extent their hecklers that can lift proceedings out of this frequently doldrumic bottom line.

Once more for the tourists

Hecklers are an extremely mixed blessing for speakers – they can just as easily lift a meeting from sluggish torpor and double its numbers as they can trivialise and dissolve an engrossing debate with a sustained barrage of crass one-liners. Many hecklers are frustrated speakers, but some have no further ambition other than to wander round being welcomed and loathed in equal measure.

Lurch, an upper-class Tory buffoon – think Billy Bunter on stilts with a snide attitude – looks back to the golden age of heckling in the eighties when he would hunt in a pack with a nasty little crew of smart-arses that included the now thankfully absent Toad and Becket. Under the misnomer The Heckler's Union, their spoiling tactics and hate-mongering resulted in many skirmishes with exasperated speakers and with the police. On several occasions it got very personal and some fairly tawdry court cases ensued. But the ultimate role model for any bile-spouting loud-mouth must be the late Lord Barker, a blustering overweight grotesque of a man who, in the late seventies and early eighties, was clearly at his 'pique'. He would strut round, pushing his way into meetings and thunder personal abuse at all and sundry, crowds of thrill-seekers trailing behind him wondering how it all might end. As often as not he would be ejected from the park and return to the entrance of Marble Arch tube station where he had a pitch selling newspapers.

© Philip Wolmuth

Lord Barker, 1978

Unsung heroes

At the other end of the spectrum there is a strain of regular hecklers who actually dignify the proceedings. These unsung heroes actually bother to ponder the previous week's arguments, they check relevant news items, research and update their information, and then return, patiently wait for a lull in the secondhand joke fest and put their questions courteously with as much genuine interest in the subject matter as they have in public debate itself. All power to 'em.

Exceptions to the role

Most speakers then learn their craft and much of their text by listening to, debating with, and of course heckling other speakers. I checked them all, taking endless mental notes. I was particularly interested in those few exceptions to that confrontational style – Ogilvy was definitely one, often ignoring the stupid hecklers or silently staring at them and raising a laugh with an expression of mock pity. Another was the now virtually solitary and silent Paul Hunt – St Paul – who refused to get embroiled in cheap banter and would dismiss any spoilers with a brief ticking off, like a tetchy schoolmaster. Paul seemed to prefer a master/novice relationship with his then considerable flock.

© Philip Wolmuth

Joshua, 1979

Where are they now?

Some I liked more for their innovation than their prowess as speakers. For pure enjoyment I watched the surreal antics of Yorkshire Dave, who would confound hecklers by answering questions with obscure cricket results, pop song lyrics or by jiggling his eyebrows. Dave disappeared over fifteen years ago and turned up at the Park on a sunny Sunday afternoon in early '99. He

Lord Soper, 1979

even spoke briefly, doing a parody of the familiar confrontational speaking style, and then rushed off saying he had a plane to catch – apparently he works as a computer programmer in California. But then maybe not. But what ever happened to Ubi Dwyer, promoter of the Windsor Free Festival; Joshua the raggedy-arsed, hippie mega-brain conspiracy theorist; Stuart the barmy baptist; and that odd-looking bloke who used to start a sentence, then contradict himself and finish off with a silly walk?

Traffle'gar Square

But the best technique I ever witnessed, which cleverly manipulated the hecklers onto the speaker's agenda, came from a youngish professorial Indian speaker. He stated that his platform had two subjects: the correct pronunciation of the English language, and the sexual significance of Nelson's Column in Traffle'gar Square. He never did get to talk about sex. He spent his time arguing, discoursing and displaying his expert knowledge of the correct pronunciation of English. Whenever he was reminded of his secondary subject he would raise his voice, and the audience's prurient expectations, and repeat his mandate with the mispronunciation of Traffle'gar Square. So triggering a correction from a heckler and the resumption of the pronunciation debate.

Lord Soper/Webster

While never a big fan of the late Lord Donald Soper, I regularly listened in on the patronising old cleric and must have learned something, watching him deal with all-comers and doggedly dragging the meeting back to its theme. Neither was I that convinced by Webster, who I considered to be an erudite speaker but a very dodgy human being – at different times, he'd spoken as a fascist, a socialist, and ended up as an advocate of Islam, allegedly 'on the pay roll of the Mullahs'.

Webster, 1978

Jim Huggon, 1981

Anarchy

Meanwhile back in the bear-pit, I was a regular in the meetings of Jim Huggon (London Anarchist Forum) where I picked up a lot of clever answers (and quite a few daft ones) to FAQ's about anarchism. Jim, with his long hair and beard, red and black costume and head full of jokes, became a bit of hippie anarchist 'character'. I especially noted his passionate tirades on the evils of work. When pushed he would jokingly admit to being an accountant, which was in fact true – he did the books for Housmans book shop and various other collectives. He took to the sticks in the eighties and I still see him very occasionally playing fiddle in the tipi field at Glastonbury and other summer festivals.

SPGB and the Marxists

I further sharpened my political edge on two Marxist-Leninists: David, a dapper little barrack-room lawyer with a pencil moustache who had an

© Philip Wolmuth

Heiko Khoo, 2001

answer for everything; and Peter, an Asian market trader, who seemed more interested in posturing Lenin-like on their high ladder under a billowing red flag. They failed to instigate the people's revolution, and like many other straight leftie apologists, quietly faded from view after 1989 with the downfall of the Soviet Union. One bunch of left-wing puritans – the Socialist Party of Great Britain – managed to brazen it out and, while the personnel may change, they have maintained a joint speaking platform to the present day. I still heckle them, and a friendlier bunch of living anachronisms you couldn't wish to meet. Meanwhile, a fresh Marxist speaker appeared in the early nineties. Heiko Khoo (who looks more Latin than Oriental) clearly enjoys speaking and he debates the issues of the day in depth and with relish. At times of crisis he is particularly good value. During the Kosovo bombing, he was one of the few people researching and updating their facts and offering thoughtful alternatives to the newsak of the media.

Just a bit of fun

As a post-punk fringe performer in the late seventies I was investigating traditional working class entertainment; and as a white anti-racist I was becoming increasingly incensed by the racism I discovered on the working men's club circuit. Many white club comedians would top a sequence of racist jokes by slipping a black stocking over their heads with holes for eyes and mouth and then go into a vicious parody of a West Indian or Pakistani. I'd been escorted out of a social club in Homerton for heckling, and likewise become dangerously unpopular at a pub in The Old Kent Road. I compared all this to what I was experiencing heckling the black and Asian speakers at Speakers' Corner. I was, for a while, in awe of the Asian Speaker Roy Sawh, more for his command of very large audiences than the actual political content of his platform. Once I was heckling him successfully in the middle of a large crowd and to prove some point he asked me what colour I was. I replied playfully "You tell you me. I can't see from here." It got a ripple but not as much as his capper "You see, always the black man has to do the work." After a couple more lines like this, plus laughs, I wanted to be elsewhere. Even my mate, my black mate, got a pertinent laugh at my expense with the old Tonto to Lone Ranger line. "What do you mean *we're* surrounded?"

Eloquence and effluence

I got even shorter shrift from David White, the eloquent Nigerian barrister, who would correct my grammar before he demolished the premise of my arguments. His devilish advocacy of Idi Amin was a lesson in appraising colonial oppression from another perspective and an intelligent antidote to the trivial white racist ravings of Peter 'England' who held equally large, if much noisier, meetings close by. 'England' looked like John Cassavetes and sounded like Bob Hoskins. He started off as an aggressive, humourless rabble-rouser but gradually evolved over many years into a chirpy cockney tourist attraction with a twinkle in his eye. His material hardly changed but the man clearly did. I used to heckle him regularly assuming stupidity – not knowing what sex or colour I was. But it was clearly his continual interaction and growing relationships with the regular black and Asian hecklers that turned him from hate-monger to genial josher.

Black slack and white racism

When any speaker uses race as a way of polarising an audience, it's cheap, even ugly. When a black speaker rabble-rouses the blacks in an overwhelmingly black meeting with familiar riffs about slavery and colonialism, while at the same time characterising individual whites in the

David White, 1978

crowd as culpable oppressors, it can create an atmosphere of suppressed violence. The white minority can feel threatened and intimidated. Clearly not as intimidated as the only blacks in a white audience at a Bernard Manning gig (where the immediate world outside is also overwhelming white), but intimidated none the less. A black crowd laughing loudly and confidently at the jokes of a black speaker in this context are not necessarily racist. What they're doing is in some way indulging in a payback ritual for the very real racism they've experienced (and many continue to experience) in their own lives. The whites in the audience, especially in the current climate of increased awareness of racism, to a greater or lesser degree recognise this, and it is this recognition – the white guilt – that double binds them and restrains their objections to any excesses. Ironically, this paternal concession creates the equivalent of an intellectual black ghetto where slack attitudes can thrive because they are tacitly sanctioned. Haroon, originally from Mauritius and a speaker since the late sixties, is a living example of this syndrome. I listen to him periodically but find his often venomous delivery and cheap rabble-rousing of an overwhelmingly black, Arab and male crowd, not offensive, but irritating. It cancels out any political lessons I might glean from his provocative defence of Western bogeymen such as Bin Laden, Gadaffi and Saddam Hussein.

Black, radical and independent

In the last few years, a far more interesting black speaker has emerged who is already redefining and out-growing the more obvious expectations. Ishmahil Blagrove is young, cool and built like an Olympic athlete. To a casual observer, he may sometimes look and sound like the next black radical demagogue but it ain't the case; any closer inspection reveals an independent and powerful speaker with a considered platform. Whatever racism Ishmahil may have experienced, it certainly hasn't made him bitter; his anger has an accurate political focus, specifically the institutionalised racism of American capitalism and its all-pervading globalisation. To his credit, he deals with the ubiquitous 'easy-target' American tourists with

© Philip Wolmuth

Haroon, 1978

increasing flair and good humour.

You are what you hate

An even more classic transformation than Peter England's retreat from race hatred was what happened to Black Jimmy, who took a basic crowd-pulling riff from the right-wing bigots and made it his sole platform. He would turn up late in the afternoon and deliver a decidedly OTT homophobic rant. Over the months his outraged descriptions of gay sexual practices became increasingly detailed and obsessive, much to the delight of a growing crowd of gay men. They had started turning up early to hear him, before participating in the then after dark Hyde Park cruising scene. The meetings got wilder and the heckling more celebratory as Jimmy's tone became increasingly ironic. Eventually nature took its course and Jimmy was (allegedly) seen drinking regularly at the gay pub somewhere behind Marble Arch station.

Crunch time

My own personal crunch-time came around that same period – the winter

The gathered church of Stuart

© Philip Wolmuth

Guru Barry, 1978

of '77/78, in the meeting of Barry Roberts. Barry, then as now, was a friendly, earnest and disarming character, a seeker, always willing to hear people out. I meanwhile was on a mission – anti-racist and anti-sexist – and fixated with updating the legacy of Lenny Bruce to embrace anarcho-feminism; and at my most pushy. I regularly abused Barry's goodwill and habitually over-contributed. As a last resort, in an effort to shut me up, he would invite me to speak. I would always decline, concealing my sheer terror with seeming nonchalance, while quietly longing to be up there fulfilling my fantasy.

Finally in January '78 I accused him of not taking enough risks, of saying nothing dangerous or forbidden. When he inevitably offered me his podium – an old milk-crate – I had no way out; I knew my moment had arrived. I confidently stepped up and delivered a taboo-breaking diatribe on free speech. In less than five minutes the police had ejected me from the park for swearing (they can't do you for stupidity or arrogance). The last words of my debut speech were: "Even this person tugging at my sleeve came out of a cunt." For the following twelve months I enjoyed considerable notoriety; I held lively meetings and managed to get myself thrown out a few more times, twice landing up in Marylebone Magistrates Court charged with language and/or behaviour likely to occasion a breach of the peace. Alex Lowry, a heckler of formidable intellect, acted as my 'McKenzie Witness' and his partner Gillian, a trainee lawyer, helped organise my defence. We lost of course – apparently the magistrates can't allow a 'not guilty' verdict, so instead they allow a moral victory. There was never a fine to pay; just being tangled up in that time-wasting bureaucracy was considered warning enough.

Barry Roberts, bless him, is still a seeker and still speaking and now known affectionately as Guru Barry. Think of an ism and Barry has probably given it serious consideration if not joined its ranks for a trial

Ali the surrealist

period. Eminently approachable and to be found speaking at the epicentre of the meetings, Barry is currently Jewish and can be heard having intriguing debates with students of Islam.

Art belongs to Dada

Another speaker obsessed with identity is Ali the resident slow-burn surrealist. Never short of a modest crowd, Ali's meetings are as entertaining and thought-provoking as it gets. I often tend to approach him on the blind side, fearing that if he sees me he'll deliberately throw me a few personal curves. He has no qualms about taking his time and speaking in riddles and confusions – it's a style that causes furrowed brows, nervous laughter and bewildered hecklers. I always spend a bit of time with Ali, he's a charmer.

Light ent's

Last but not least, a long-term inmate whose presence is difficult to ignore at Speakers' Corner is the gregarious Martin Besserman. If size of audience is the mark of a good speaker then Martin is simply the best. On many occasions when I've been reluctant to speak, Martin has encouraged me, offering me his ladder complete with a crowd of a hundred plus. He has a regular clutch of speakers who benefit

© Ishmahil Blagrove

Geraldine

from this gift, including Sexy Geraldine who, in her own way, is attempting a female version of Martin's platform – not an easy task. Martin is almost an institution. He has been publicly chatting up women, putting down men and showing off to everybody for at least 25 years. Apart from a tabloid-style interest in the fashionably topical, his material has hardly changed over the duration, his meeting serving as a living archive/nursing home for weary old jokes and routines. Every Sunday, for hours on end, he attracts big lively crowds of tourists and entertains them with his playful narcissism and tales of sexual conquest. He is assisted in this ritual by a contingent of the more oddball regulars and hecklers. They stand in the front of his meeting, a baying chorus, delivering their tawdry heckles and feeding him lines while somehow basking in the reflected glory that is Martin the unlikely swaggering super stud.

Alternative

From May 1979 my 'full-frontal anarchy platform' at the park became less important to me and I started catharting and arguing politics as an alternative comedian on various rock and cabaret stages. I had to unlearn a lot of bad habits, but how to censure hecklers was never one of them. From that time on I've often used Speakers' Corner to develop and try out material for the stage, knowing it will have been test-run in the harshest of conditions.

Truth

Almost everything that is said at Speakers' Corner I never hear, although I may have heard it before. Almost everything that happens I know little about, apart from what I pick up on a very unreliable Chinese whisper service. The rest is my experience, my observations, my lyrics and opinions. This is the journal written from my diary. I'll try and keep to the truth. It is of course highly subjective and I've been extremely selective; I've added things of interest, and omitted things of no interest to me or that might confuse, and every now and again, just to keep you on your toes, I've bunged in a bit of information that is complete and utter bollocks. But see the irony in it – the truth you get from me is much the same as any other truth you might get.

THE JOURNAL

Sunday 4th June 2000

I arrive on my bike, late in the afternoon, carrying a lightweight aluminium stepladder over my shoulder. I stop, a couple of hundred yards short, and watch the crowds of people milling about and shouting in the distance. If you didn't know about Speakers' Corner and happened upon it by chance, from here you'd probably think there was a demo kicking off or maybe an obscure illegal sporting event taking place. To me, it's all too familiar. I've been coming here since I was a kid in the fifties, but I still get a bit of a frisson on arrival.

The End is Nigh(ish)

Apart from a flying visit in February earlier this year, I haven't spoken at the Park since October '99 – over eight months ago. I was fairly regular up until then, throughout 1999 and most of '98 – I was on a mission, my platform being a variation on The End Is Nigh and based around the Millennium bug. Negligent technocide would have been such a pertinent end for the burghers of Western materialism, so geared to short-term profit that they skimped on the computer software and left a couple of expensive

noughts off the end of the date. Bosh! Thank you and goodnight! Wheel in
the next attempt at a civilisation.

I believed in it passionately and conducted large and lively meetings, as
well as small and intense ones, covering a wide range of associated doom
and gloom subject matter from self-sufficiency to global conspiracy
theories. I got quite obsessive about it, ranting on at great length, citing
information gleaned from internet news groups and stuff I'd picked up in
conversations with fellow Jeremiahs. I was so convinced I even left home
and went and lived in the hills. But it didn't happen of course, and I was
horribly, horribly wrong. Speakers' Corner regulars, and there must be
hundreds of them, have got long memories, and they're not going to let me
forget this one.

Artist in residence

Since then I have developed a new mission based around a London Arts
Board funding application that I playfully submitted in May and which, to
my surprise and delight, was accepted. Now I am both personally committed,
and contractually obliged, to try and change the confrontational nature of
the way meetings are conducted at Speakers' Corner, and to offer my
services as an advocate heckler for those who wish to question other
speakers but who are either too lazy, shy or intimidated to do so. For the
next couple of months I am in research mode and then, from the first
Sunday in September, I will be an Artist in Residence – one of a thousand
artists in a thousand places. I wonder what other the 999 are doing?

On the wrong track

I make a brief diversion and enter by way of Speakers' Corner proper, the
area adjacent to the Marble Arch one way system. Very few speakers use this
space nowadays; about ten years ago there was a realisation that the traffic
noise was too much, and so most of the speakers gradually moved further
into the park where, ironically, they now completely block the cycle track for
eight hours every Sunday. Not everyone made the move. Lord Soper spoke
in exactly the same spot every week, for decade upon decade, right up until

he died about three years ago. Paul Hunt is the only regular speaker still occupying this two acres of tarmac, and he's had the same patch for almost three decades. To call Paul a speaker is probably stretching the definition, seeing as how he just stands on his milk crate in silence for most of the day. Occasionally he'll fall into conversation, but only with those he deems worthy of his time and energy. Milk crates incidentally, not soapboxes. I can't ever remember seeing a soapbox here, or anywhere else come to think of it.

St Paul

I cycle round and stop in front of Paul.

"Afternoon Paul." It's always worth waiting to see if he replies. Slowly a smile forms

"We're still here then?" He closes his eyes. That's it – the audience is over.

"Yeah. I got it horribly wrong. Laters."

God! How many times am I going to have to say that today? It's an odd feeling this – being pissed off that the world didn't end. At one stage I had

St Paul, 1980

a fantasy of returning here in a Mad Max style vehicle, shouting 'I told you
so' through a loudhailer at any survivors. But I'm better now, quite
optimistic. On a good day, I reckon the planet's got at least 25 years left –
enough to see me out.

I park my bike and ladder close to The Socialist Party of Great Britain
meeting. Nick, an SPGB stalwart, a bit of a plodder but decent bloke,
wanders over and says, "The world didn't end then?" I thought he'd never ask.

"No. Well spotted Nick. No. I got it horribly wrong. Sorry if I caused you
any inconvenience." He seems quite forgiving. They won't all be.

"Are you going to speak today?" he asks.

I act all nonchalant and reply "Maybe. Depends how I feel." Which is
short for 'I'd really like to, but now I'm here I've gone all wobbly and I'm
desperately looking for any excuse not to go through with it.'

Preparation

I generally find it very difficult to psych myself up to speak. It's not like a
stand-up comedy gig where there is a specific twenty minute slot at an
agreed time. Here, it's all down to me and my own willpower, and maybe a
sense of duty to some nebulous public expectation. Neither am I part of a
group like the SPGB, who share a platform and commit to a speaking rota.
My most favoured method for getting in the mood is to wander round and
listen to a few other speakers and heckle a bit first; then, if I still can't crack
it, I seriously warm up on a Christian.

By the time I've strolled around and met a few more locals, I'm getting
fed up with the millennium bug and even more sick of listening to myself
apologising because it never kicked in; but I am learning how to eat shit. I
change tack however, when a speaker, Guru Barry, recognises me on the
edge of his meeting and taunts me with "So what happened to the end of
western civilisation?" and twenty people are waiting on my reply.

"I saved the planet, didn't you hear? Because of my warnings, they got
their act together and it didn't happen." It gets a bit of laugh, but it's not
the way I want to be dealing with it. "I'll be getting a mention in the new
year's honours list" another ripple, but I must stop this now. I've clearly got

my wits about me. I must be honest, make a public apology and take it from there. Who knows where it'll lead. Hopefully I can soon put the whole thing behind me.

Another new Messiah

There's between fifteen and twenty speakers, only a few have big crowds of a hundred plus, half of them have small crowds of no more than a dozen, and some (mostly the obscure religious sects) have no actual audience at all. One of these has been pointed out to me by several regulars. He's a new addition to the ranks of wannabe Messiahs and is already thought of as decidedly dodgy. This sounds like a job for 'Advocate Heckler'. He's stood on a plinth, facing a non-existent crowd, bellowing, Bible in hand. He occupies the favoured spot of Heiko Khoo, the Marxist speaker, who draws my attention to the cause of people's unease. Standing awkwardly either side of the preacher, holding up banners with unreadable hand-written slogans, are four slightly vacant acolytes – two men and two women of various races. These poor souls are probably having second thoughts about what they're doing here. They've probably committed themselves to a short spell of speaking later on, and their only way of breaking the ice and hearing their own voice in public, before actually doing it, is to shout out the odd 'praise the lord' or 'Amen' to punctuate the main man's monotonous foghorn.

Advocate heckling

I move in closer and stand directly in front of them. I'm on my own. This is a very odd set up. There's a lot going on here, this could be a movie. We have here several very unhealthy relationships. The preacher is an uptight, thick-set, East European in his early forties. Dressed in grey slacks and a white open-necked shirt, he oozes latent aggression and stares into the middle distance shouting biblical quotes in broken English. Despite his haunted look and the fact that he's made no attempt to make eye contact with me, I still find him intimidating and it's not that difficult to imagine how he might channel all this anger into charisma. I don't like him, he's scary – dangerous even – a good role for Robert De Niro. Listening to him for a few minutes, I get the idea he reckons the world is going to end shortly. The irony is not lost on me – you are what you hate – but unlike me he doesn't believe the answer is a grass roots anarchist revolution. He's on a 'make your peace with God or burn forever in Hell' tip.

I decide to treat him like a deranged gunman in a rooftop siege situation, and opt for the softly softly approach. "Can you hear me Dutch? Put down that Bible and release the four hostages."

He doesn't bat an eyelid. He doesn't hear me – just carries on shouting – but it gets a laugh from the little crowd that's gathered, and so does: "Have you ever given serious consideration to recreational drugs? I don't think it's a listed sin." But I don't get into my stride until I start playing to the crowd indirectly by addressing his minions with gambits like: "He'll be a lot better when he sorts out his personality. You just hang in there." "I s'pose when you get to know him … eh? As a friend like? … No?" and "Can anybody join or is it a closed community?"

Heckling is, of course, much easier than speaking, and doesn't require that I sustain anything or follow it through, or at this level, even think it through. An oriental woman, who is loyally minding his suit jacket while also holding up a banner, looks straight through me. Her vacancy has more to do with not understanding the language, rather than being brainwashed or spellbound. What is going on here? I'm just contemplating how I might communicate with her, when I'm aware of the next heckling shift – the arrival of Irish Chris.

"Burning in hell is it? Well, you've picked a nice a day for it." Chris is the bane of all Christians and has developed a heckling style to suit the terrain; it simply involves repeating snatches of text and throwing in his own comments. He walks around muttering aloud, directly beneath the speaker who is still shouting and still dysfunctional. I take a step back and observe, not wanting to get into a heckling double act with Chris – with two of them now talking at once there's little space for much else. And anyway, this is Chris's chosen speciality subject. "Ah! Almighty God! And just where did he come from?"

Rung rusty

I fetch my ladder and set up close to where I've been heckling, and consequently pick up a few people without attempting to bark a crowd. Danny, one of the SPGB speakers, comes over for some friendly banter by way of saying 'hello' and very soon I'm chatting to a bunch of people I haven't seen for a while and inevitably I'm again apologising for the Y2K bug; but it's interesting and intelligent. I'm glad to be doing this. People react well to hearing a speaker admit they were wrong. The truth disarms them. Someone suggests that a lot of my ideas have got apocalyptic conclusions; and there is a jokey consensus that I've probably got a doom gene. A few others own up that they might have one too.

Other people's lives

I notice a more than subliminal change in the soundscape, like a faulty extractor fan has turned itself off: the Robert De Niro preacher has finished speaking. Shortly after, he and his cowering little flock walk past me. The oriental woman returns his jacket. He takes it without acknowledging her. He is distracted, dictating to the others how their banners should be folded. Other people's lives are exactly that – other. I have to remind myself I'm an artist doing research, not a saint or a social worker. I watch them as they leave and suddenly they take on the appearance of an average family group going home after a relaxing day out in the park.

Speaking and chatting

I find it much easier to talk to a dozen or less people because I'm not really in speaking mode. I quite enjoy it as well. Any more than a dozen and I have a dilemma that I've never quite resolved: my ego dictates that I curtail the conversational-style contributions from the core group up the front and start addressing the larger meeting, assembling unnoticed, around them. This gets confusing for everybody, especially when the crowd dwindles again to conversation size and I'm still ranting away, playing to the park. In the course of an hour I screw up several times. At one point my meeting melts away to nothing – they're probably pissed off that I can't make up my mind. I decide I'd prefer to chat for the rest of the day and resign myself to talking to small meetings.

'No' to ritual humiliation

I spend another hour chatting, speaking and making interesting mistakes. I stick to a game plan of encouraging serious discussion and attempting to deal with hecklers humanely and without resorting to ritual humiliation. This in no way inhibits them from dishing it out – on the contrary. They're an odd bunch, hecklers; tell me about it. Some of the most unattractive human beings I have ever encountered have been hecklers. See Toad, Lurch and Lord Barker.

Sufi chanting.

I'm just about to pack up when a tour guide arrives with a large gaggle of Dutch teenagers and I make all the girls laugh by mimicking the cool swaggering of their dominant male – a fifteen year old Adonis. A crowd gathers, drawn by female laughter. They soon find another focus however, when an old mystic with a long white beard and flowing purple robes who has been asleep in a deck chair behind me, hears the wake-up call and decides to teach the girls Sufi chanting. He looks the part and has a delightful, impish quality about him. I can hardly start heckling him, so I join in and encourage what's going on. For ten minutes or so it turns into a party. Abandoning my ladder, I get into conversation with the tour guide and I finish my day in anorak mode – swapping historical information about Speakers' Corner and Hyde Park.

Sunday 11th June 2000

During the week I see a late night telly documentary on the Learning Zone about the origins of Methodism, and I'm very taken with the gigging schedule of John Wesley. He rode all over the country on horseback, sometimes doing three solo shows in a day. I'd love to do that. That's just the sort of regime I need to get me up to speed. It reminds me of an unfulfilled plan that I was toying with ten years ago. I was going to cycle round the country doing an eco-warrior speaking tour. But it never came to anything. I got a puncture one night in Finsbury Park and had to walk home. It wasn't the puncture as such; it was the mess I made trying to mend it. That did for the idea.

I arrive at the park about 4pm. A scruffy bearded sixty year old man is stood in silence on a crate where St Paul usually stands. Paul meanwhile is seated on his crate a few yards away, head in hands and looking a bit despondent. They both stare blankly into the middle distance. Very odd, very Samuel Becket.

"Afternoon Paul. Found a new follower then?" Paul acknowledges me with a nod and a wan smile but says nothing. I stand there astride my bike also motionless and silent trying to capture the mood. Somewhere this man has something to teach me, but I don't know what.

A family of passing tourists stops to observe the tableau. I feel as if I'm part of a kids' prank – tricking people into looking at the sky when there's nothing to see. As it happens they don't follow our eyeline. The kids look at their parents and the parents look at each other. Now there are seven us. I'm first to break ranks. "Enjoy" I say and I cycle off.

A few minutes later I am chatting about the quality of the meetings with a small group of speakers and regulars. The basic subtext is that we all share the same fantasy – we'd love to be able to sustain a large audience without pandering to the lowest common denominator. Bryan, a white Zimbabwean who is often at the centre of these intense little leaderless discussion groups but usually talking about world economics, is encouraging me to come and speak on Saturday when there is only a handful of speakers, no compulsive hecklers, and the mood of the meetings is more receptive. I find this difficult to understand because the Saturday scene revolves around Martin Besserman. Martin is as larky and tabloid as Bryan is earnest and serious. But seeing is believing, so I agree to do a Saturday in the next few weeks.

I warm up by heckling hecklers who are trivialising a pleasant young Christian lad who has positive things to say about liberation theology, but I turn on him when he starts getting emphatic about original sin. But I did give him the benefit of doubt.

I don't have a favourite place to speak but I prefer not to get too close to the other meetings but not so far away that I'm isolated. Also I'm not one for being surrounded so, like the majority, I tend to speak with my back to the railings. Other speakers have entirely different considerations and someone who likes being in the thick of things might come and squeeze in next to me. If they get too noisy I eventually move. No one has any rights, but some speakers do turn up at a particular time and speak from a particular location as regular as traffic noise, and I've never yet heard tell of a turf war.

I park my ladder on the junction of the walkway under the plane trees and shout at people to go away and leave me alone. A small crowd gathers. They start talking among themselves in a language I can't fathom and then move on, leaving me back at square one. In eighteenth century rural England John Wesley wouldn't have encountered this sort of rejection. Eventually Danny the socialist comes over and by way of a kindly comradely gesture starts a noisy argument with me, and very quickly a less fickle English speaking crowd gathers.

It's certainly an improvement on last week. The high point is my demonstration of the dynamics of confrontation. By raising my voice a couple of notches and repeating what might easily be construed as inflammatory statements – "You, a black man, say that to me, a white man?" and "Women! That is so typical of a woman" – I immediately pull another twenty people in to my meeting, much to the delight of those in on the stunt.

But I'm not messing about experimenting this week, I'm attempting to sustain a crowd and quickly get on to my main fail-safe subject – the work ethic. '95% of work being unnecessary, undignified, demeaning, dangerous, or simply causing more problems than it solves', is a topic I run with. Asking individuals what they do for a living is fertile ground, even (or especially) if they lie. 'Cleaning up dog shit from the park' leads to a rant about people's lack of meaningful relationships with other human beings; 'litter picking' leads to demanding

Free speech, 1993

everyone should pick up their own litter and that manufacturers be made responsible for their packaging; 'net curtain salesman' (Martin) for encouraging a society of Peeping Toms and grasses; 'a washing machine salesman', with contributing to built-in obsolescence; and 'a clothes designer' of pandering to the whims of fashion. This one can run and run. I barely touched on the possibilities. I received a round of applause at one stage, springing from the statement that my only rule in life is 'Get in good company' but I think it was a bunch of friends celebrating a birthday. Anyway it inevitably leads me back to the work ethic and the sort of company you find at work and how, even if you do find a good friend or fellow spirit there, you have no control over whether they are sacked or promoted. To be honest it's a bit hit and miss at times with crowd numbers fluctuating anywhere between ten and thirty, but I haven't been crass or trivial and I've made a point of treating hecklers with more respect than they get elsewhere. I finally notice the numbers in the meeting dwindling because I'm exhausted and no longer alert to finding replacements by manipulating passers-by. Tired and hoarse after two hours of speaking, I step down and a tourist couple applaud, making the whole thing suddenly feel like an endurance test that I've failed on a show of hands. Did John Wesley have gigs like that, I wonder?

I'm invited to have a drink and talk 'Speakers corner.com' with a bunch of regulars and I'm just packing up to go, an afternoon's worth of ideas and events like a tossed salad in my head, when I am approached by a studious looking young woman who I've noticed in the meeting earlier. She has black horn-rimmed spectacles and is dressed in a pinstriped three-piece suit, but her style is not smart-city, it's more fun-punk – purple leggings and army boots with pink laces. Her whole look is teetering on art. Turns out she's a librarian from Dublin, first time in London and on a weeks holiday. We leave the park together chatting. She has an astute take on the difference between male and female modes of self expression – men demanding attention and women attracting attention. I leave her in Edgware Road and it's only later in the pub when Martin is trying to get the conversation away from 'politics' and on to 'girls' that I realise that I'd just been chatted up. I know I've been pretty relaxed about sex, love and relationships of late, but I was unaware that I'd completely lost the plot. The next thing I'll discover is that John Wesley had groupies.

Sunday 18th June 2000

I'm getting into a routine on Sunday afternoon. First off, before I even leave home, I have to overcome that sinking feeling I have about speaking. This is often physical as well as psychological, and even though I've been up and about for a couple of hours and had a big breakfast, I still have to force myself to make the effort to go and do it. Finally I cycle to the park about 3pm. Sometimes it can be as late as 4.30. On arrival I check St Paul, then I go and I stash my bike and ladder on the wrong side of the railings near Ali or the SPGB. Then I wander round, socialise and engage in some creative heckling. Finally, and it might have taken an hour, I reach that moment when I decide to mount my ladder and speak. Compared to this moment, everything that follows for the next two or three hours is a doddle.

Detour

The routine, of course, varies and today, en route, there's a detour when I recognise an old mate and stop. She invites me to share a spliff and we walk along the Bayswater Road giggling at all the unintentional kitsch art hanging on the railings. I'm in a gentle mood by the time I cycle up to St Paul and to my surprise he's friendly and oddly communicative. Paul doesn't share my view that Speakers' Corner has the potential for change and could produce something extraordinary out of all this human interaction. He reckons that nothing changes here. The speakers have nothing to say and they are saying it to people who aren't listening. I point out to him that he never listens to any of the other speakers, so he would be the last to know what's occurring. He maintains that there is nothing of any consequence occurring. End of argument. So, by this logic, until events prove otherwise, 'the master' is right. Huh!

I ask him to give me a thought for the day. He smiles, reaches into his pocket and produces a book, thumbs through and reads out a line of text to me. I'm quite pleased with myself; this is a breakthrough. I've had more communication with him today than I've had in the last two years. I cycle away from him musing on whether it's my receptive stoned state that has opened him up, got him talking and sharing his thoughts ... his thought for the day! Already, I've forgotten it. Something about wisdom – which in my case I have not got. Short-term memory loss – the curse of Mary Warner. I am not worthy.

A short while later I'm in a big crowd watching me old mate Dr Stewart improvising with whatever comes up. He's a delightful extrovert – tall, slim and black with cropped peroxided hair and an infectious sense of play. He's a fellow cabaret performer and also a Covent Garden street entertainer, majoring in robotics and mime and I know that he must be here working up some narrative skills for his stage act. What Stewart lacks in content he makes up for in technique and attitude. He mocks, mimics and mugs with fluency, his timing is impeccable and there's an easygoing humility about the way he welcomes the interruptions of hecklers – laughing at their jokes and getting into ironic competitive rallies with them. This man has the grace to attend my performance workshops as a student, but I always consider him a guest tutor because I personally always learn so much from him.

© Ishmahil Blagrove

Doctor Stewart

Next, by way of saying hello to Red Danny, who is addressing a small crowd, I launch into a public argument with him. It's that sort of a relationship. I listen to him for half a minute, over-simplify what I believe he believes, and then feed it back to him. As far as I choose to understand it, Danny and his group have a small-beer vanity publication, the monthly Socialist Standard, plus a weekly platform at Hyde Park with which they are attempting the political education of the entire international working class – some five or six billion people. Once this is achieved there will be a convenient crisis in capitalism, when free and fair general elections will be held everywhere, resulting in a landslide victory for the SPGB. And, er, that's it – a bloodless revolution. Oh yes, and I personally will have to take my turn cleaning and maintaining the sewers. The born-again Christians seem to be offering much the same deal, except with them the sewers are on fire and I'm stuck down there permanently. The banter has attracted a few punters and I leave him with the line: "I can't stand around here talking to you loser groups, I've got some effective sedition to lay on the populace."

I spend a further ten minutes listening to Ishmahil and note that for the first time his audience (of over a hundred) has almost as many white people as black. Two years ago I thought Ishmahil was a bit slack, but now I enjoy listening to him. He's dropped much of the guilt-tripping tone he once had without losing any of the impact of what he's saying. His attitude still has righteous anger and arrogance, but it's less threatening and is now tinged with deliberate parody. He's also structuring some very witty routines to advance his devil's advocate celebration of all things black and critique of all things American. I am becoming a fan.

Dreams and nightmares

After thirty minutes I get my stepladder, find an empty, desolate space and brace myself for starting without an audience. I could make it easier for myself – I could go round and tell a few people that I'm starting – but for research purposes, I'm doing it the hard way and learning to explore and play with the situation. But there is a nightmare scenario and it goes as follows: Stood on the ladder with no-one listening, everyone sees me with no audience – alone and friendless. For the most part, they don't know that I have only just appeared and have yet to start speaking. They see an empty meeting and assume that I'm deranged or deadly boring or that I'm being ignored for some other justifiable reason. They consequently give me a wide berth. Now the space around me has increased. People are out of reasonable earshot and avoiding eye contact. None of them will make the first move. I attempt to attract them by raising my voice and performance. Everyone sees a rowdy gesticulating speaker who is being ignored – they give me an even wider berth. I am isolated, ostracised and experiencing total rejection at *the* venue of live communication.

This is one of the tapes running in my head as I start shouting, "Unclean! Unclean! Unfunny! Keep away from this meeting – there's something dodgy about me."

Finally I hit the open space in front of me with the legend "Wrong drugs! Wrong drugs! Football hooligans take the wrong drugs."

Football fans tanked up on lager have disgraced themselves on the continent. Soccer pundits and television presenters have admitted to feeling ashamed of being British. It's topical tabloid subject matter. People turn and smile and within a few minutes I am talking to a dozen or more, and for the next hour, whenever it goes below that number, I simply raise my voice a tad, repeat the mantra and top up the numbers. I use lager louts as a route to talking about cannabis and its myriad uses and delights, and the fact that it will be an important pillar of an anarchist economy. The subject shifts through a gamut of related topics – soft drugs and hard drugs, legal drugs and illegal drugs, the media, national identity, drunkenness and sanity.

I don't plan what I'm going to speak on. I am generating a body of work, repeating and developing it over the weeks. It's mostly in my head and not yet written down – ironic rabble-rousing, lists of demands, riffs, routines, explanations, anecdotes, examples, answers to frequently asked questions and endless gentle and not so gentle put downs. I'm dipping in, using what I need, and adding to it.

And I'm cracking jokes. Jokes from my stand-up act. In twenty years as a stand-up comedian, I've generated another body of material around these same subjects – a parallel archive – and some of it is gradually finding its way into my public speaking oeuvre. Some of it started here and is finding its way back. Some of it makes the move effortlessly …

"Soft drugs lead on to hard drugs. Oh yes. Know it. I started off on marijuana and within a few months I was on the hard stuff – tobacco!"

"How can you trust a newspaper – a newspaper that always has the same amount of pages?"

"My Country? If this is my country, then I want my three n' half acres Now! Alright I know it's only about two acres when you do all the sums. But basic trade union negotiating strategy – always demand more than you're willing to accept."

... Some of it doesn't, however. Some of the more reflective stand-up material makes an untidy transition to alfresco finger-wagging oratory. Problem is, it's honed, heightened and embedded in routine; crafted for a different medium – intimate cabaret. Often, when I'm public speaking, a seemingly appropriate (if untried) stand-up routine will occur to me. I'm capable of rattling off sizeable chunks of this stuff, just so long as I can remember the gist and the first few words. I'm not the sort of diligent artist who does preparation and who's going to dig it all out beforehand, reselect what works and reject what doesn't. That would take aeons; there's so much of it. Most of it works and I'll take a chance with the rest. My performer's instinct is to spontaneously launch into it without thinking, it's only then do I realise that I'm totally out of control and performing a piece involving subtle microphone biz, dialogues, or integral mime and movement (not conducive to being performed stood on the third rung of a decorator's ladder). It's this sort of omelette that happens next. So it goes.

Someone mentions MDMA and rave culture and I automatically cut to the 'soccer hooligans on ecstasy' bit. A pertinent stand-up routine, which starts off smoothly enough with some interesting information:

"In the '90s, footie fans started taking ecstasy in the rave clubs on Friday night and then took another one for the match on Saturday afternoon. Consequently there was a marked reduction in violence on the terraces; and what's more the fans were appreciating the game from a totally new perspective."

I could have left it there. But I don't. I can't resist the punch-line. A very mellow soccer hooligan, E'd off his tits, slowly and triumphantly raising his hands in the air and blankly stating: "Go-al! ..."

Some people laugh, not as much as a cabaret audience, but they do laugh and I'm seduced by it and continue with the routine. The silly voice. The hands waving slowly. I have seamlessly erected a fourth wall and now I'm stuck behind it.

"Go-al ... Go-al ... Did you see man? It was a ... Go-al."

My instinct is that there's a punchline along here soon and everything will be alright. I'm now performing a pause-laden conversation between two softly-spoken lads on their first ecstasy trip, stood directly behind an imaginary goalmouth. I'm quietly panicking – I haven't performed this routine for at least three years, One lad is doing slo-mo hand movements, swaying in celebration, the other is mesmerised and motionless. I'm delivering it on automatic while my mind scurries ahead to check how good the end might be and if it's worth the candle.

"... Like the whole fractal lattice work of the net, yeah, did a rhomboidal shift yeah? (I skew my hands) Know-what-I-mean? Did you see? Did you see?"

"Nah man ... Elsewhere ... I was watching the after-image of the keeper ... the keeper ... the keeper ..."

People are bemused; they're wondering what I'm doing. For me, after I've recovered from the dismal failure of it, it's an interesting and revealing mistake, which I don't stop to analyse, although I've got an inkling it's a tad important. Later, on reflection, I see that it's a fundamental – a Fourth Wall thing. Now, it's a mistake and a mistake I know I'll make again.

The crowd is dwindling but I'm not too concerned. It's been almost an hour and I'm feeling quite satisfied that I've improvised with a seemingly fresh and topical subject for so long. Red Danny turns up on cue and I begin to collude in my half of our unspoken mutual heckling arrangement. I'm not happy doing this, and even though I know it's working, I'm thinking it's a bit cheap. I'd much prefer to be sustaining crowds of a hundred plus; drawn towards me and transfixed purely by the quality of my lyrics and my sheer animal magnetism. In reality I'm having a fake slanging match with a mate, as a ploy to keep my crowd numbers in double figures.

More pertinently a group of young back-packer types, who have been sat down at the front of the meeting since the beginning (something people do in the hot weather), don't like it either and look as though they might leave. They're an important section of the crowd for me, less fickle, less interested in the ranting or the heckler interaction and much more likely to stick around for the thought-provoking, 'current Zeitgeist' stuff. I express my feelings.

"I can't be arguing the merits of socialism with you Danny. As far as I'm concerned we had all that out in the late eighties. And you lost. I've got to get on with the serious anarchist business of decoding the Zeitgeist. To yer average browser in the ideological market place, all that Socialism stuff sounds very yesterday. Interesting analysis but lousy conclusions."

Danny doesn't like this at all. How much he is role playing I'm not sure, but he gets quite shirty. He has his supporters too, and the ensuing low-brow sloganeering and esoteric quibbling sees an exodus of the studious youngsters in the stalls and a build up of regular hecklers bunging in their two penn'orth, plus a few thrill-seekers who wrongly believe there's some real aggro going off. Danny leaves in a huff when I answer everything he says with "Yesterday Yesterday! All fucking yesterday!"

I finally get onto my regular fail-safe theme of the work ethic, which involves some ritualistic banter with hecklers. It is while I am screaming at a particularly pedantic heckler, turning away, throwing my hands in the air and pleading to the gods, that I catch sight of a large group of fifty or more sprawled on the tarmac near Soper's old haunt opposite St Paul. They appear to be a school group with a couple of teachers, but it reminds me that on lazy sunny Summer afternoons last year, a black American held regular, similarly laid-back gatherings in that same spot. I can remember being impressed by his quiet charisma, anecdotal approach and the fact that his large receptive audience – including that international back-packer contingent – appeared to have been gently seduced, disciple-like. I return to my heckler vaguely inspired and changing tack I question him softly.

"What's your name man?"

"Jeffrey." He begrudges.

"Jeffrey ..." I ponder Christ-like, "... Jeffrey, I shall call you ... Pedant!"
I spend another half-hour experimenting with trying to build a crowd but
without resorting to alienating any more of my potential allies. I'm
regretting the way that I've trivialised the argument with Danny. And okay,
I've been brittle and inauthentic at times today, and that stand-up stuff
going decidedly avocado didn't help, but I'm less ring rusty than I have
been of late, and although I'm still nowhere near in control of what I'm
doing, I am beginning to enjoy myself.

Also I'm sustaining a little group of mates and comrades – Damien,
Jonathan and Andy the anthropologist who's written a thesis on Speakers'
Corner; they hang round supportively for most of the meeting and later we
might go for a post-park drink. At the other end of the spectrum, I've also
picked up a few rather gormless and antagonistic hecklers who, for reasons
I've yet to fathom, seem to have attached themselves to me. There's always
at least one of them stood up the front giving me grief. Perhaps they're a
given. Perhaps a meeting at Speakers' Corner can't function unless the
awkward squad has a presence. Perhaps there's a nit-picky gripey little
archetype that certain personalities tend toward and inhabit whenever
there's a perceived vacuum? Perhaps I should be grateful for any attendance
I get. The head count of these modest gatherings at any given time,
although rarely slipping below ten, neither sustains for very long much
above 25.

Before the meeting breaks down into a friendly chat with the comrades I
explain publicly and non-exclusively to everyone that unless they want to
meet me at either Stonehenge for the Solstice 5.30am on Tuesday, or in
the Green Futures Field at Glastonbury Festival on Sunday, they won't get
another chance to heckle me in public until a week next Sunday.

Sunday 2nd July 2000

Speakers' Corner is treated in a extremely cavalier fashion by the Hyde Park authorities who throughout the year, and particularly in the Summer, stage occasional Sunday concerts – anything from boy bands to popular classics – on the adjacent few acres of open park. High fences appear over night, and the decibel levels during the gigs are often unacceptable. The only semblance of a speakers' union revolves around Heiko Khoo, Martin Besserman and Ishmahil plus a few others, who are responsible for the www.speakerscorner.net website; but I don't think we have a representative sitting on a committee or anything like that. The mind boggles at the idea of organising this lot; a consensus of grumbling is as democratic as it gets. Today the police have decided that speakers will have to occupy the original area close to the Marble Arch one way system. By the time I arrive St Paul has already left, probably unhappy with the invasion of his territory. Most speakers have discovered new pitches mostly round the edges of what must remind many of a large school playground. Some are still moving around unsettled and trying out new spaces. There is also an extra contingent of police including a mounted officer I recognise from previous weeks. He's wearing black jodhpurs, knee-high leather boots and has a neat moustache – guess what his nickname is? Today he seems doubly stressed and officious and people are complaining (to each other) about his interference in meetings.

My plot this week is to keep it low key and conversational, welcome the disruptive heckle as a cry for help and encourage contributions to foster a serious debate. But I'm feeling playful and I still have the nagging notion of playing the charismatic orator.

I set up slap in the middle of the tarmac – a lone figure – chanting loudly with irony:

"Bigger cages! Longer chains! Better consolation prizes!" "Bigger cages! Longer chains! Better consolation prizes!"

Andy comes over and gives me his thesis on the sociological value of

Speakers' Corner. We start chatting and a small crowd gathers. Gerry joins us, but he's not staying. I'm disappointed; he's a well-read political radical from Northern Ireland, always a good man to have in a meeting. He tells me that he's off to Regents Park to listen to a world music concert. He particularly wants to hear a Croatian choir and invites me to join him. I decline. I've only just arrived, he's been here most of the day and now he's off for a few beers and then a concert. I like Gerry – a man who knows how to enjoy himself.

There are hecklers who play the devil's advocate game better than some speakers. I haven't been long started when I gradually realise that the chirpy old cockney in a flat cap stood up the front asking awkward questions is a serious wind-up merchant. He has an increasingly outrageous line of thinking, which I've been treating like sensible contributions to the debate. He reckons that the introduction of legalised abortion in the sixties resulted in a subsequent missing generation of cockneys that were replaced by immigrants to make up the numbers. This lateral line of low flying dodgy logic starts all manner of arguments in the meeting – a women's right to choose, racism, immigration, NHS, housing, and by far the most favourite topic 'what constitutes a true cockney?' I'm not in control of any of it and to make matters worse, after about half an hour, I notice the flat-capped instigator in the middle of another meeting, while my crowd are still at each others throats debating his agenda.

I finally get back in control by playing it large and for laughs. It's mostly frivolous, but I'm happily besting hecklers and wise-cracking to a lively crowd of about thirty when the mounted cop rides passed slowly looking as if he's just sucked a lemon. There's an immediate air of expectancy as if I'm supposed to say something. Instead I look at him and then corpse, shake my head and say:

"Too easy." Or maybe it was "Nah, far too easy."

Whatever. This is roughly the line that gets the laugh.

"I heard that!" Says 'im on 'is 'orse "... and If I hear you swear again, you're out of the Park."

There is a spontaneous uproar. The witnesses to the fact that I didn't swear are all bearing witness.

'im on 'is 'orse

I appeal to the crowd "Did you hear me swear?"

"No!" They shout, and they carry on shouting lots of other things. I am six foot four and stood on the third rung of an aluminium decorator's ladder, suddenly I'm aware of company immediately behind my head. I turn and I'm face to face with a horse, a magnificent dapple grey, big soft eyes, flared snorting nostrils and chunky teeth. Above and beyond is Leonard Rossitter doing an impersonation of Adolf Hitler.

"You've been warned! Once more and you're out."

One thing about me that I love is, I rise to the occasion. All I need is a cheering crowd and to be vaguely in the right, and I'm there – I'm on it. I just automatically go for it. I'm excellent value on demos. I'll be brilliant at the revolution. You see. I look him straight in the eye and say "Outta here!" He starts to say something but I simply interrupt him with clear staccato instructions.

"No! Outta here! You! And yer horse! Now! Outta here!"

Then once more emphatically "Outta here!"

And he goes. Backs right off. Right out of here. Course he does. I mean think about it. He's gonna have to write the report not me. It doesn't always work of course. At Glastonbury a couple of years ago I took the initiative in an abortive drugs bust and ended up sat in the mud with a face full of CS gas. But that was the exception.

I turn round to the crowd and suddenly discover there's two hundred, maybe three hundred of them flocking round hoping to witness a cheap spectacle. The ghosts of baying mobs and demos past, all stalk this turf – mass assemblies of chartists, Victorian rioters, and all those famous and infamous last words uttered by the condemned on Tyburn gallows. Hard acts to follow. Always address the now. Charged with adrenaline, I'm on it. I laugh acknowledging the crowd's vicarious motives and shake my head contemptibly.

"You bunch of thrill-seekers."

They laugh. Perfect! Already they're warming to me. They've got high expectations. I can feel it coming off them. This is one of the largest crowds I've ever addressed here and they're still arriving – due to some police activity behind me. I'll ignore that until I'm disrupted. I've got enough to be thinking about. Large crowds can be monsters. I could have said 'You fucking thrill-seekers' that would've been elegant (even if the new arrivals didn't get the joke). But so far I'm in the right and the police are in the wrong and I like that. Best not to have tossed it away on a one-liner. I decide to bring them up to speed on the situation and give them some local background.

"First off, who heard me swear at 'im on 'is 'orse? Nobody. Because I didn't."

"Oh yes you did."

"No he didn't. It was me."

"You're always swearing. You've got that syndrome."

The thing about big crowds is everybody wants a chunk. The meeting's full of hecklers and they're all trying to make a name for themselves. Some of them are deliberately swearing from the safety of the crowd. Hecklers too have an important archetype to inhabit – the lone shaft of wit and common sense from the back of the crowd that exposes the demagogue.

"If you hear anyone swear at Speakers' Corner and you're offended by it, bless, then you can go and tell a policeman. Then, and only then, can they take appropriate action. What we can't have here is the police going round being offended on their own initiative."

An honest citizen asks a question. "Since when has it been against the law to swear?"

A heckler answers immediately. "Since fucking ages ago."

I answer the question in the role being ascribed to me by the monster. I've read the books, I've seen the documentaries, and I've downloaded photos of the General Strike from the website. I'm the local hero rabble-rouser up a ladder. "Language and or behaviour likely to occasion a breach of the peace ..."

"The Queens peace."

The nitpickers are out in force too.

"Whatever. The 1928 Public Order Act. Brought in to curb the racist ravings of Sir Oswald Mosley. But they can just as easily bust you for talking about making love and naming the bits."

"Bandits at four o'clock!" Warns a regular.

I turn round and there's a stern-faced matronly policewoman looking up at me. She speaks quietly and firmly.

"Utter crap! You don't know what you're talking about. Any more trouble at all from you and you're out. That's your final warning."

She's right of course, I'm talking bollocks. The laws here have all changed since I last fell foul of them twenty years ago. Nowadays, it all comes under the Hyde Park Bylaws and the police have complete discretion. There's another minor hubbub going on with some of my regulars and local troubleshooters, who I only now recognise, are all standing close by in support. But I can't work out what's exciting them. Meanwhile the crowd wants to know what's been said.

"I've just been informed that I don't know what I'm talking about. Which is correct. I have been talking rubbish. No she's right. I was just winging it – making it up as I went along. It doesn't make me a bad person."

They laugh but they are disappointed.

"Get a job."

Whether this is a daft heckle or a prompt, I'm not sure. But I notice the police moving away and realise that the thrill-seeker element in the crowd will leave with them, especially since all I've done is to convincingly mislead them about the law of the land. I decide that rather than start the revolution, I'd best just talk about it and find a way to segue to 'anarchy' and 'the work ethic' and see if I can't hang on to some of this crowd.

"What do I know about the law? I'm an anarchist."

The truth is of course that the police have always operated in much the same way here. It's always been at their discretion. Whenever I was arrested in the past, they never produced an offended citizen. They always made that bit up. Although I am thinking this, I don't express it. I'm too busy working out a face-saving strategy. Alex Lowry places a slip of paper in front of me. It reads "405/128 – crap." The numbers of the two cops – the mountie and his female boss – and the reminder that she had said 'Crap'. Oh, yes 'Utter crap' I'd let that go – very slack. That's what the comrades had noticed. Seeing Alex, I get a déjà vu. It was Alex who had been there at my side twenty years ago when I was campaigning for my right to use sexually explicit language in context. I don't want to go down that route again. Law courts and their proceedings are such an energy drain.

"I'd like to thank the police for drawing your attention to the anarchist meeting."

When they realise that there's not going to be a fight or an arrest, half the crowd dissolves almost immediately. But I seize the opportunity and try and hang on to the remaining hundred or so, and for the next half hour enjoy manipulating and playing with the largest meeting I've had for ages. It finally dribbles away back to my current norm of twenty, when we discuss the episode with the police in a bit more detail. Finally I repeat my dictum that no revolution ever took place without the police and the army on side. So in the interests of furthering the anarchist cause, I close the meeting and approach the mountie in an attempt to build bridges with the constabulary. He is still mounted and talking to a foot patrol. I introduce myself, tell him that I'm sorry that we got off on the wrong foot, and reiterate the fact that I never swore at him and that he must have misheard what I said. All the while I am talking he listens as if he's under orders to do so. He makes sure that I've finished before he replies.

"You were in the wrong. I was in the right. There's nothing more to be said."

I report back to the comrades, who think I'm mad. Someone brings me a coffee and they leave me to drink it alone.

A gaunt, ashen-looking thirty year old immediately buttonholes me. He looks as if he hasn't slept for three days and talks in animated articulate bursts interrupted with despairing sighs followed by calming silences where he appears to be monitoring his own breathing. I feel like a contestant on 'Name That Drug'. I suspect he's coming down off of something very lively and he's had a toke of something very soothing but I'm no expert. He starts quoting me 'Get in good company'. 'Get in control of your own life'. It transpires that he's a squaddie, been one for fourteen years since he was seventeen. He's done the lot – Belfast, Bosnia, The Gulf, Kosovo, and now due to fly off to Africa (he's not sure what country) on Tuesday. He's been in London for a week on a serious binge, and if he doesn't go back to barracks in Nottingham tomorrow he'll be officially AWOL and, more to the point, he's just heard me tell a receptive crowd of a hundred people to take control of their lives and not go into work in the morning. What I actually said was:

"If you're life's in a rut, if you hate what you do to earn a crust, then it's about time you were creatively irresponsible. Tomorrow have a lie in, leave it 'til about 11am and then 'ring in well'. Pick up the phone, ring the boss and tell him. It's a lovely day, the sun's shining, the birds are singing, I feel great and I'm not coming in. Ever again. Screw your fucking job."

He's got the gist of it and I get the idea that he's going to take me at my word. Normally I'd shake his hand and tell him to be lucky. But there's more and it feels horribly real. When he was stationed in Germany eighteen months ago, his wife was going slowly mad in the official armed services housing estate and so she took to coming down to the barracks and making a nuisance of herself. One day she got hold of a repeat rifle and went berserk. Her shooting spree failed to kill or injure anyone and just when it seemed it would all end in extreme embarrassment, she turned the gun on herself. He watched it all happen and had to live with the consequences. From what I could make out, the tragedy made him a pariah and any mates he might have had quickly gave him a wide berth and left him totally isolated. Rather than continue with the British Army's psychiatric counselling regime, he decided to put a brave face on it and pretend he was over the worst. He had no family and no life outside the Army.

I didn't know where to start. He'd grown increasingly paranoid telling me all this, and when I made a tentative attempt to talk him through his options he stifled a sigh, put a brave face on it and walked away. "Be lucky." I heard myself say.

A bunch of young Muslims ask me if I am going to speak. I'm used to this. What they are really saying is 'Do you fancy an argument?' And 'Yes' I usually do. Some of these kids want to know how they are perceived in the world outside of their own community and are itching to wear their faith on their sleeve and get some feedback on whether it suits them or not. My opinion doesn't matter that much, I'm just a loony in the park, but they've got to start somewhere. Of late, I've turned these exchanges into a symbiotic relationship and I've been seizing the opportunity to play the wise old guru. I must admit to over-doing it sometimes and sounding very condescending, but I'm working on it. I'm not really up for it after my session with the disturbed squaddie, but I nevertheless mount my ladder and start chatting to them.

They move on after a few minutes leaving me with an audience comprised almost entirely of very straight looking black-suited East Europeans only two of whom speak English. I quickly discover they are from Croatia and when I ask them if they can sing, a large ebullient middle-aged man is pushed to the front and then with his deep baritone voice leading them, they let rip with an impressive ten minute rehearsal before going off to entertain Gerry in Regents Park.

Sunday 16th July 2000

I arrive about 3.30pm, on foot and without my ladder because a mate's picking me up later and we're going out. St Paul is unusually cheerful when I ask him for his thought for the day. He tells me "Think before you speak." And I say "Good!" immediately, without thinking. My first laugh of the day and it's unintentional.

Today's plot: Sustain a debate from whatever comes up; encourage plenty of contributions from the floor; have a friendly chat rather than play it large to the park. As for the hecklers: 'disturb the comfortable, comfort the disturbed' and even try and involve them and find the positive in whatever rubbish they come out with.

Pick and run

By 4pm I've heckled Ishmahil, returned Andy's thesis and found myself an unwanted milk crate. I haven't thought through anything in advance as I mount my dais. I'm even unsure how I'm going to start, but I'm stood there gathering a crowd by telling them to go away. It works. In fact anything works, so long as you have promise. Someone says he saw me on the telly and actually knows all the details of a comedy sketch show from the mid-eighties. I tell him it was a bit of casual work I did one afternoon back when, and I regretted it – I got £200 for two hours work and wished I'd stayed in bed, and could he please not talk about it again. But it's the spark I need and I'm off on a rant that's been brewing for a while. I tell them that in two years time they will all have their own live television channel with back up archive. Forget fifteen minutes of fame; soon anyone and everyone will be able to strap a camera to their forehead, suspend a mic from a harmonica holder, plug into the net, do their own voiceover, and narrowcast on-the-spot, real-time coverage of their own life – a live video diary 24 hours a day. Over-enlightened societies will make it a human right.

Future shock

That gets things going. I've touched on this theme in previous weeks and the wackier I make it sound, the more fruitful the debate. It's the other side of the Millennium bug story; this is the future shock scenario that sees the new media expand until we are globally totalled with it – info'd out.

Although I've talked it through a few times in stoned late-night brainstorms, this stuff doesn't exist yet as a coherent sequence, never mind material. I've got some riffs in my head; but it's just wacky ideas for the most part – I'm repeating other peoples opinions, I've got no firm angle of my own, a vague scenario, nothing more. I keep hitting blocks when I can't remember the correct language, logic or technical details. I'm being heckled by people who know what they're talking about. I'm quietly pleased by this but less happy about being exposed as bullshitter. For the first time this summer, I wish I had access to some ordered notes on my chosen subject – the equivalent of a stand-up comedy set-list.

A6 montage

I always carry an A6 notebook – I've got several. Or, bottom line, the blank side of a flyer folded to A6 – I've got dozens of them. Whatever, none of them are of any use now. I only use them for input; they exist only for their blank spaces, not for their content. The content's in there somewhere but it would have to be deciphered. Lead pencil, betting shop biro, fountain pen, felt tip, back, front, arse-up, every which way; block caps, copperplate, scribbled and scrawled; my notes are a chaotic rag-bag of abandoned acronyms, addresses, word play jottings, contact names and numbers, web sites, street directions, recommended book titles, overheard one-liners, rhyming couplets, half-written reviews, tentative song lyrics, herbal remedies, gig, demo and event dates, redundant set lists, memorable jargon, workshop notes, topical jokes, anagram doodles, re-spun news items, first impressions, famous last words, scribbled messages, and drug-induced spontaneous downloads from my brain. Most of it is boldly crossed out – data, info, knowledge and wisdom, already keyed-in and filed on the word-processor at previous monthlyish intervals, when I also get to tear out pages and maybe end a tome and start a fresh one. It's a wonky system and it often fails me, especially at times like this. I desperately need an administrator for the left-hand side of my brain. I make a public announcement for the job vacancy. There are no takers.

Luckily there's several computer buffs and they're staying with it, extemporising on the subject and answering each other's heckles. Conversations spring up and I go into chair mode. I spend time listening. I even produce the remnants of my current notebook and make scribbled entries in a personal shorthand on available space.

After about an hour or more I take a break. What has been a meeting of a dozen or so hardly dwindles, and people stand around chatting. I ask them to hang on to the milk crate and I wander off for a piss and to check out Heiko before he leaves. He's been urging me to enlist in his internet training scheme – for all my mouthing off about cyberspace, my understanding of the practical nuts and bolts of assembling a web site is embarrassingly limited – this current display of the gaps in my knowledge has been a pertinent reminder. When I return there are still half a dozen people stood round chatting.

Two other regulars have joined the meeting; Jay and Alan are both semi-uniformed Hyde Park litter pickers. Jay is a twenty year old laddish bright spark and most of what he says to me is a gentle wind-up and I have to have my wits about me. One week he's going to join the army, the next week he's a minor league gangster. This week he is entertaining ideas of anarchy which he reckons – and I'm responsible for this understanding – combines the best of both previous life choices. Alan is ten years older, over-qualified for the job and enjoys an intelligent discussion; he's also a meticulous litter picker. So not only do my meetings have a strong class base, they are also very clean and tidy.

Collectives in waiting

I intend to carry on where I've left off, but as soon I re-start the meeting I find myself arguing the merits of Anarchism as opposed to Socialism. Once again I characterise Socialists as anti-revolutionary – always finding excuses to stop things happening. I condemn their 'utopian blueprint' approach to the revolution as doomed to end in bureaucracy and totalitarian hell. I repeat what is now a piece of public speaking material.

"Let's start the revolution! Now! We can't be hanging about waiting for the enlightenment of the entire international working class. They can catch up later and when they do, we will have a network of social experiments as living examples for them – communes, collectives, associations and cooperatives, already on the go, making mistakes and ironing out the local difficulties. You socialists best stay away from these Temporary Autonomous Zones, you might like what you see. You might be persuaded to change – come over to the other side and join the living revolution."

I bung this last bit in especially for the SPGB followers, one of whom, Toby, has recently done exactly this – defected to the anarchists. He stopped speaking on the SPGB platform a few weeks ago and has now set up as an anarchist speaker.

I follow this up by waxing lyrical about various groups I have stayed with around the country, particularly the Exodus Collective who several years ago squatted a derelict hospital, formed a housing co-op (which acted as their landlord) and then started paying their Housing Benefit essentially to themselves and enabled them to fund and build customised living quarters for all their members. Eventually they bought the property and then went on to expand and squat a disused farm and repeat the operation.

I'm still only chatting, but I occasionally raise my game (and my performance) and kick it out to the masses beyond the immediate meeting of no more than twenty. There are moments when serious public speaking feels more of a possibility and that image of John Wesley returns to me. Why him? Why not Fidel Castro or Jesus Christ?

'Disturb the comfortable, comfort the disturbed'

I inevitably tangle with my regular hecklers – Jeffrey the Pedant and an odd little character called Albert who, despite his friendly demeanour, is an appalling reactionary. Albert seems far from disturbed, although his opinions are very disturbing. His misogyny, racism and homophobia are expressed with the air of a perky apology for the way things are. Why these oddballs should be attracted to me is probably to do with the fact that I let them have their say and don't put them down as soon as they open their mouths. In many other meetings speakers and hecklers use personal abuse as the first line of merciless attack.

Whatever is immediately obvious is a target: looks, age, height, grey hair, lack of hair, untidy hair, national identity and regional accent. All have to be defended and justified before the content of what's being said is considered. The more familiar the target, the more entrenched and distorted the caricature. I once met an Iranian patriarch in his clothes shop in the East End, which he ran with his wife and daughters. We spent many minutes trying to recall where we'd previously met until eventually we realised it had been Speakers' Corner, where he and his brother, who were demonstrably close, were briefly known as the Iraqi homosexuals. My meeting must offer welcome relief from all this sort of gunk, and consequently I'm lumbered with more than my fair share of tiresome oddballs.

It sez 'ere

Acts of worship

A little before 6pm a group of about thirty Muslim men gather on the adjacent grass, form two lines and kneel in the approximate direction of Mecca. Then, under the guidance of one of their number sitting a few yards ahead, they begin synchronised prostration and prayer for several minutes. Some of the Christian groups have similar acts of gathered worship at various times during the day, usually small groups in a circle with bowed heads around a solemn speaker reading a sermon or saying a few words of prayer. I'm intrigued by this phenomenon and find it serene and dignified and the complete antithesis to some of the behaviour that goes on in the religious meetings where Christians and Muslims scream at each other brandishing copies of their holy books as if they were demo banners or improvised weapons. What I want to know is: are they the same people? No member of my meeting knows or cares and I now become more interested in observing different people's reactions to the acts of worship. The hardcore atheists scoff, others are uncomfortable with the subject, but most of them find it irrelevant. George, who sounds as if he might be a pupil of Albert, wants to know that seeing as how they know where it is and how they love it so much, why can't they all just fuck off back home to Mecca? I tell him that he, personally, would probably be more at home in Kabul with the Taliban given his views on women, censorship and homosexuality. But this is lost on him. He's got it into his head that Mecca is the capital of a country called Islam where Muslims come from. The question inevitably follows and it comes up a lot: Why is Speakers' Corner so full of religious fanatics? I answer this in a half-arsed way: What I try to say is that people are spiritually clueless and have lost touch with each other. I begin to explain my recent experience at the Summer Solstice at Stonehenge where several thousand of the most extreme characters I ever cross paths with, spent eight hours in tentative striving for spiritual communion. But this, especially under fire from hecklers, proves even more unworked-out than my description of cyberspace. I hear myself talking, and the tone of my voice sounds like one of those has-been celebrities who advertise stairlifts on daytime telly, so I jump off the crate, kick it into touch and call it day.

Saturday 22nd July 2000

A plinth and a possibility!

At last I respond to Bryan and Martin's invitations and efforts to get me to speak on a Saturday. I arrive about 3.30pm and I'm surprised to see St Paul, stood on his crate, occupying his familiar place and with no audience as usual. Through the trees, a hundred and fifty yards away, I can see Martin speaking to a sizeable crowd. There's no other meeting. I'm immediately struck by a sense of the bizarre. What is it with these two? Both are hardcore denizens, having rarely missed a Sunday in decades. Now, seeing them both here putting in overtime on a slow Saturday, I get to pondering on their sanity. And on mine.

Paul is cheery, thoughtful and remarkably sane when we exchange greetings, although he is emphatic that I don't speak anywhere near him. I set up in what is becoming my favourite spot, under the plane trees along the fence and round the corner from him and facing Martin, who's diagonally across the broad walkway.

It's a very big park and there are clearly very few speakers, I feel obliged to explain about Sundays.

"Free Speech! Free speech every Sunday! Offer now extended to Saturday for a limited period. Get your free speech here."

A dozen people gather round in an atmosphere of 'Let's check this out'. They are mainly foreign tourists visiting the park; only a few of them are aware of Speakers' Corner. We are a bonus and they seem to have a genuine fascination with the idea of a free speech forum. I explain the background to the place, dwelling on the more outrageous and overtly political information – the stuff that I know about. I answer questions about the legal situation with a brief resume of the police powers and some lively descriptions of their recent arrogance. Well, I'm not the tourist information board am I? Martin is right, it is a much better atmosphere without the regular spoilers.

The crowd gradually swells – there's not the usual fall-off rate with only one other distraction (two if you count Paul). I settle down and chat to them, discovering that many of them are part of a job lot of Scandinavian drama students – Danish and Swedish mostly – regrouping here after a day's sightseeing. More interestingly, I discover that only a few of them are the usual stereotypes – the two scruffy bohemian middle-aged women, the bloke that looks like a bank clerk, the lad in the wheelchair and the tweedy matron pushing him – are all Scandinavian drama students as well. Of course they are.

"I've been getting it all wrong, I've only been seeing part of the picture. Previously, when I've seen a bunch of foreign students, I've thought 'that's all of you'. But I was wrong wasn't I? I never saw beyond the stereotype. I didn't think to look around at all the other people going in the same direction. I didn't know they were all foreign students as well, only less obvious – student incognito."

I point at a few borderline cases. "Are you a student?"

"No."

"Are you a student?"

"No."

I've already eyed-up my third. A been-around tanned jet-setter couple has dwelt briefly at the edge of the meeting. There are some people you just have to talk to if you've got the licence. I look straight at the woman.

"And you. Are you a student?"

"A student? Yes ..." She says in a stilted sexy Mediterranean accent

"... But only of a little corner of life."

The couple laugh with each other and walk off. It's probably a film quote, but it worked. Everyone is smiling. A precedent has been set. This is where observations are made and witty epigrams are exchanged.

"You are an actor?" Asks a young blonde male stereotype, unaware that the answer to his question will lead inexorably into my current obsession and the core of my artistic identity. How long have they got I wonder?

"No, I'm not an actor. Are you a member of a theatre audience? No. We have no such contract. We are not acknowledging any theatrical convention.

There is no suspension of disbelief. Already we are talking – there's no fourth wall. Any of us, me included, can leave at any time. You were just passing by and I'm a loudmouth up a ladder in the park."

I'm getting into this – these people are perfect casting to hear all my theories about performance, even if some of it's decidedly wonky in places. I start off with an explanation of the difference between an actor and a cabaret performer and, although not everyone's up to speed, the Scandinavian drama students are devouring it. The audience has halved, but the remaining dozen or so are doing more than listening. They are participating, asking me to clarify concepts like the 'fourth wall', not because they don't understand them, but to make sure we all have the same understanding. This is not really Speakers' Corner; this is civilised conversation.

"So, you are a performer?"

I am of course, but I'm also average Joe Citizen expressing his right to free speech. I hedge my bets.

"Not a performer, as such. No. But I might well use some performance skills and I certainly have the artistic agenda of the radical performer – to demolish redundant clichés."

This grabs their attention. Good. Because I've got an untried rant I've been toying with …

"Our language, our thinking and our behaviour is infested with cliché. Clichés are the given. We live in a world defined by the past. We are surrounded by all the clichés of yesterday. When we wake up each day it is still yesterday! Still yesterday until all the clichés of yesterday have been identified and then confronted, scrutinised and rigorously tested for truth and relevance."

Yeah, that's the gist of it. Ironically I'll soon have some quotable clichés about cliché. Now I get into a discussion about how reinforcing clichés creates stereotypes and I start quoting relevant clichés from chaos theory.

"'All form tends toward the archetype; the archetype itself has no form.' Example: This tree is a London Plane. No two leaves are the same. Each leaf is different. They vary in so many ways depending on location, age and health. They are not the same, they are self-similar, but no one leaf can represent the size, shape and colour of all the leaves. In the same way, none of you is representative of a Scandinavian drama student. The stereotype is the enemy of individuality."

This next bit comes right off the top of my head.

"Deeply embedded in the thinking and behaviour of the culture are clichés based on lies, on religious intolerance – on yesterdays fear. The cliché left unchallenged can harbour taboo."

In the discussion on taboo I come out with.

"In a smug liberal society, to believe that there are still taboos is taboo!"

"So you are an artist?"

I won't deny it. I'll answer the question with a question.

"Then what is my art form? What sort of cabaret artist is it that stands in a public place and improvises a discussion from a casual remark? No. I'm a loudmouth up a ladder in the park. There's no fourth wall – temporary or otherwise. No walls at all. No play. No script. No set-list. No spotlight. No

Martin Besserman, 1978

microphone. No Admission fee. No exclusion. So most definitely no contract with the audience. Have you seen the audience at Speakers' Corner on a Sunday?"

They haven't.

"No mercy! I spend at least 50% of my time arguing with hecklers. A discussion like this is virtually impossible."

"You have a stage?"

"This is not a stage. It's a focus. It indicates that I've got something to say and I'm willing to keep up one end of an argument."

"So why do you do it?"

"Because, what we have here ..." I say this investing my tone with increasing gravitas. "... is the possibility of the pure form."

From my vantage point I can see that their disparate colleagues are gathering to leave. They have collected a few from the teashop and a further bunch from Martin's meeting and now a group of about fifteen are approaching. And anyway, this has all got far too cosy. Right, let's see how

© Zac Zacharides

Martin Besserman, 2000

much they've learnt.

"Truth is, I'm an anarchist troublemaker dedicated to decoding the Zeitgeist. And there are times like the present – times of solar turmoil that occur every ten or eleven years, when the sun spot activity effects human affairs. When the world's news bulletins show iconic images of ordinary people ransacking police headquarters, occupying airports, radio stations and television centres. Times like now. Oh yes, it could happen anywhere on the planet – Harare, Zimbabwe or at home in Copenhagen, and it could happen here too."

I pause and corpse into a smile to remind them that we have no contract. I'm not an actor. Whatever the nature of my performance, I am not asking them to suspend their disbelief. Quite the opposite. I might be a madman, a visionary, a trickster, or just a deluded out of work comedian. But I am for real.

"You might see it on the news. When the mob spills from the park and blockades the junction of Edgware Road and Oxford Street. I'll be there with them. I'll be the one standing on the street furniture, pointing at McDonalds and The Bureau de Change, shouting in a strong manly voice and with clear diction 'Storm the reality studios!' Someone's got to do it."

I don't smile this time, that might be a cue for applause or some form of completion and that would be inappropriate. They are about to leave before hearing the whole story, so they can just think about it for a while. Some of them are smiling. The new arrivals aren't sure what's been going on, but I was right about their direction. They amble past picking up their stragglers and, after a brief flurry of thankyous and goodbyes, I'm left with four people listening to me.

"In the park there's no contract with the audience. There is no fucking audience."

"In the park there is no swearing."

It's the stereotype blonde Scandinavian drama student. Turns out he's Anglo-Dutch and a full-time cook in Docklands. And he's been paying attention.

I draw attention to Martin, who still has a sizeable crowd. We watch him dismount from his ladder as he dissolves his meeting.

"See that. He finished his meeting while he still had a substantial crowd. I could never do that. I'd be lucky to have that many people listening to me in the first place; and then to just 'Up and leave them' on a whim. That's how we define machismo in these parts."

And it is. I can't resist throwing in a coda of pure sour grapes.

"Too bad he's just spent two hours talking bollocks."

Martin gathers his stuff, shoulders his ladder and wanders towards me with some of his flock following behind. Then, to gently rub my face in it, he passes the time of day with me and starts bantering until I've got a crowd of thirty or more. Only then, does he go for his tea-break. Probably done a days work before I got out of bed, as well.

A stumble through cyberspace.

Martin has introduced (and left me with) the subject of Big Brother, the cult on-line, lock-in, television docu-talent show. Martin's secret, apart from the small matter of 25 years consistently honing his craft as a speaker, is that he's a real punter. He'll happily spend hours gossiping about which contestants in the show will get laid first. Me? I'm a snob. I'm much more interested in the ramifications of new technology on the future of the media.

With the assistance of the bright young Dutchman, I re-establish the mood of participation and we start exploring the cyberspace scenario from last week, only this time without the Sunday rowdies and nitpickers.

"How many people here have a telephone? Nearly everyone.

"A television? Almost everyone.

"A personal computer? Well over half.

"Email address? Nine. About a third.

"Personal Website? Four.

"Photos on the website? Three.

"Video on the website? None.

"Bandwidth. We're just waiting on the bandwidth. Scenario: In two years time you will all have your own narrowcast web station. Your own television channel? A third of you for sure. The merging of telephone, television and computer technology plus bandwidth equals a revolution in the media and perhaps beyond."

Audience numbers are starting to dwindle mainly because people think it's some sort of sales pitch. So I have to explain otherwise by doing the 'Speakers' Corner' bit, and the 'loudmouth up a ladder in the park' bit, again. It works and now I've got twenty people and they're all listening. I want to share my understanding of the current state of the technology and I've just remembered a pertinent little intro. It would work best from a cabaret stage in front of a room full of comedians, but I've decided not to do that anymore, so it'll have to be here.

"Intellectual property is theft! That's my line! Nick it and I'll sue? In fact. Don't even think about it"

It's mildly appreciated. I continue without breaking my stride. "A mate comes round my flat late one night, opens his expensive new laptop computer, logs on the net and says 'Give me a song title and make it as obscure as you like.' I'm not feeling particularly adventurous so I give him one I'd like to hear. It's Alright Ma by Bob Dylan. Within two minutes he offers me a choice of 27 versions and plays me a bootlegged version I've never heard before. He then plays me an obscure version of Old Man River by Paul Robeson that he's discovered, but with the line 'I'm tired of living but scared of dying' replaced with the less poetic but more overtly political 'I'm tired of living but I'll keep on fighting' and snarled out with rage. Powerful stuff. But I digress. Point being, this whole organisation has evolved from a bunch of pop music buffs having met on-line and got into swopping tunes. The result being Napster, which is simply thousands of people making their record, tape and CD collections available as common property."

Ron, the Dutchman, explains and updates the current legal situation with Napster, emphasising the panic that the music and entertainment industries are in with these developments. I like Ron. He incidentally hasn't got any of the technology but apparently his absent girlfriend has. She's a cocktail waitress.

I pick it up again moving the subject along to where I want to take it.

"Today – music. Tomorrow – television programmes and feature films. The archives of cyberspace are infinite. Soon people will be making their video collections available as common property. But let's re-wind. Big Brother and it's ilk are the state of things to come. Primetime television is currently low budget presenter-led goo plus acres and acres of repeats. In terms of their output, some nights the BBC television centre need only have one person on duty. For most of the night, they actually don't even need a light on. Just a link person occasionally sat in front of the camera with a video machine. 'That was Only Fools and Horses and now tonight's film which contains strong language and scenes of violence, it's Apocalypse Now.' Again!"

I slipped behind a fourth wall there, and into a stand-up comedian's snapshot characterisation. I only just got away with it. Would it have worked on a Sunday? Probably not. No suspension of disbelief in the park. I could get into bad habits speaking on Saturdays.

Meanwhile back on topic I am trying to complete the whole diatribe and get to my conclusion, which I consider to be a set of optimistic and visionary ideas. But it's difficult. I still have to make some iconoclastic statements which need explanation, and of the dozen or so people listening only one, Ron, has been with it from the beginning of the subject, and now he's just gone off to get us both a cup of tea. Sod it – I'm doing it for myself and as a rehearsal for some future Sunday when the time is right. The gist of it goes like this (with a few clarifications and repeats):

"In two years time, with millions of on-line narrowcast web stations going out live, television as we know it, will be finished. The BBC's main role will be renting out secondhand footage. That's why there's currently so many programmes based on showing old film clips. They're preparing for the inevitable and advertising their range of archives. Only little tasters though, They won't show the whole piece, it could get pirated. The BBC may survive by hanging on to the licence fee, but ITV meanwhile, and Channel 4 and 5, Sky and the rest, They're really screwed – what chance their advertising infrastructure? Forget-it-time.

"Meanwhile, back in cyberspace.

Logging on to a website will mean tuning in to a live television channel. At present a website is a list of local archive, links and maybe a chat room. In the future a website will be live 24 hours a day, and the archive will even include live output from a few hours previous. Data, information, knowledge or wisdom. Your choice. As the virtual world embraces and dominates everything, we will enter Psycho-cultural Babel. We're well on our way already. Even among long-established communities, families, groups of work mates and friends, people might speak roughly the same language but in terms of choice of information, local argot, cultural reference and psychic identity, those people are becoming strangers. Too much information? Too much choice?"

Now I have some more original thought.

"'Pick and mix information'. I had a bloke in my meeting recently thought Mecca was the capital of Islam, the country where Muslims come from. New clichés for old. Convenience information. Shit! Man! Some people have chosen infocide – they look at nothing else but porn or football all day."

I'm saying most of this in a gentle, sharing way – I'm not trying to be overtly messianic. But then, for some reason that I trust, I say with more than a hint of anger.

"But more pertinently, most of you don't know what I'm talking about."

It's horribly true – there's actually more people listening now, but I've lost some stalwarts from up the front who I'd been conducting a dialogue with. That's probably why I'm angry.

Ron arrives back with a warmish cup of tea, bless him, and I explain about the absentees.

"We'd spent quality time together but they had to go. They were late. They didn't know they'd coincide with a loudmouth up a ladder in the park. They thought they were taking a short cut."

I even repeat some of the good bits that he missed. He likes 'infocide' a lot, after I've explained it again.

Inevitably I start to hear myself from the newcomers perception – phrases like 'Psycho-cultural Babel' and 'infinite archives of cyberspace' must sound bewildering if not disturbing. I look at the expressions on their faces. They must think we are some weird sect prophesying end times. And in a way I rather like to think we are.

"We are a visionary sect that believes that when our species built the computer it was attempting to build a facsimile of the human brain. When it developed the internet it was constructing the first knockings of a facsimile collective unconscious – just stacking the shelves with all the shit. The dominance of the virtual will both separate us from our traditional communities and tend to spuriously unite us with inappropriate spectacle, celebrity and event. But do not despair brothers and sisters …"

I'm going gently into parody evangelist now.

"… There is light. There is a flipside to the virtual and its fragmentation and false gods. We believe that there will be an equivalent paradigm shift at the other end of the spectrum. A paradigm shift in the quality of human communication itself – how we relate with each other in RL. RL – that's internet talk for Real Life! Any questions?"

There is a pause, and then someone who hates pauses says:

"Do you come here every day?"

I should finish at this point. But I don't. No sense of local machismo. I'm still standing there answering trivial off-topic questions and I start losing them steadily. It's all very polite with 'thank yous' and 'see you tomorrows'.

There's a subtle, if major, drawback to speaking on a Saturday. The continual turnover of the audience is worrying me like it never does on a Sunday; and on a Sunday the turnover is greater. Today, I have been overly concerned by how I am being perceived. At first I simply recapped some local details to put people in the picture. But their lack of that sort of information isn't the real problem. It's the information they have about me that is missing. On a Saturday there is no familiarity. Sometimes, they don't even know what I'm doing, why I'm here. I feel strangely anonymous. On a Sunday, I'm part of a whole circus – the context is clear. I am essentially speaking to a meeting at least a third of whom are regulars, even if some of them are regular adversaries. Their heckling and occasional name-calling actually helps me to continually re-establish who I am. I can define myself often in quite subtle and profound ways simply by the way I respond to their jibes and arguments. I am also being defined by my allies, especially by how I deal with their support and excesses. For instance, my occasional censuring of some of the comrades for their mindless anti-police sentiments and my insistence on the fact that any decent civilising revolution must have the police and army on-side, says reams about the sort of lateral thinking that I stand for and am capable of. Today I have had a very unfamiliar sense of self, without the benefit of a constant re-establishing of my identity through arbitrary third parties using convenient shorthand. As I flit from one spacey aspect of a possible future-shock scenario to another, nobody knows who I am or what I believe. For this crowd I could as easily be an actor as I could a nutter. Clearly what I am is a very naked and vulnerable loudmouth up a ladder in the park.

Albert turns up just as I'm finishing; maybe I could have done with him earlier. He starts complaining about 'Arabs' to the remains of my meeting who have also just arrived themselves, and most of whom (unbeknownst to Albert) are westernised Palestinians. I stay just long enough to hear him discover this fact and start digging a hole for himself.

Sunday 23rd July 2000

Arriving an hour or so earlier, I witness different speakers and different hecklers. One day soon, I must start at dawn and see the whole day from start to finish. Anyway, at 2.45pm on a lazy sunny afternoon, poor old Heiko is having to deal with a relentless stream of articulate tosh from arch heckler 'the Appalling Lurch'. Like many other speakers Heiko has realised that because 'the Appalling Lurch' is so preposterous, simply laughing at his excesses finds common ground with many in the crowd. Today, the upper-class giant is wearing baggy blue shorts to match the grossness of his opinions. I just *have* to join in, but I don't want to be obviously crass. I seize the first opportunity and laugh at him as soon as he opens his mouth to heckle. He stops in mid-sentence and looks at me with theatrical disdain. I corpse into another laugh and say:

"God! The human species is wonderful isn't it? It's just so diverse."

I leave listening to the laughter but not to his reply, which sounds petulant and gets less of a response. So early, and already I'm carving notches on my ego. Blonde Ron from yesterday follows me out of the meeting and introduces me to his girlfriend. They've been there for hours and have been waiting around to meet me and now they are leaving.

Doctor Bulgaria

I move on to Simon – Doctor Bulgaria who is speaking on the Open Free Speech Platform to quite a big crowd. When you get to know him a bit, he makes a good deal of been-around-done-a-lot sense; but in speaking mode with a crowd in front of him, he suffers from Martin Besserman's influence and indulges in barely ironic racial slurs and cheap gags. He does however amuse me with his version of a sex education lecture and given his supposed qualification as a gynaecologist, his craggy appearance, lugubrious manner, rasping voice and thick accent delivering deliberately ponderous broken English, it almost qualifies as a stand-up comedy act. I

Doctor Bulgaria explains gynaecology

spend ten minutes listening and laughing and then heckling when he starts
his anti-Arab put-downs. He's a bit sheepish when he recognises me, as if
I've somehow caught him out.

The Suit with the Bible and Drill Sergeant

Meanwhile there is bedlam around one of the main Christian platforms
with what I learn is a ritual double-act performance by a familiar black
preacher, always dressed immaculately in a dark suit, collar and tie, with
Bible in hand, and the American Drill Sergeant, a lumberjack type with
beard and plaid shirt. They stand, side by side on a high ramp, rabble-
rousing their fellow Christians and baiting the Muslims with the religious
equivalent of 'Come and have a go if you think you're hard enough' and
'You're gonna get your fucking heads kicked in'. There's a crowd of over
two hundred. Up at the front, a dozen or so outraged Muslims are waving
their arms in the air, shouting at the speakers and flourishing copies of the

Koran. An equal number of Christians are jeering these hecklers and cheering-on the platform; open copies of the Bible can be seen above their heads with fingers pointing at bits of text. The rest of the crowd is pretty noisy as well. A lot of them are non-partisan – simply regular hecklers and thrill-seekers joining in for the entertainment value. Their tone is heavily ironic but nonetheless spirited. Towards the fringes of the crowd, among the gobsmacked tourists and sociologists, are fashionable young Arab women stood alongside women in yashmacks and old Christian couples in their Sunday best, all trying to comprehend the scene before them. I watch this bizarre spectacle for ten minutes, heckling occasionally trying to embarrass the platform. But nothing I say can top what is actually going on.

Myth has it that the Drill Sergeant once dressed up in drag – a cloak and yashmack – and pushed his way to the front of a Muslim meeting and heckled the speaker in a high-pitched voice.

Christian preacher

A clear and present danger

Meanwhile I learn that various complaints have been made against the uptight mounted police officer. Not only his disruption of my meeting a few weeks ago, but also other incidents on the same Sunday, including riding his horse into a Muslim meeting and creating a clear and present danger. I haven't seen him since. Good. Let's hope he's been grounded and given lots of forms to fill in.

Fear of failure

Before I speak I again experience that fear of failure to pull a crowd, of being rejected.

I thought I'd put that one to rest. I decide that whatever this negative feeling is, I am going through it and out the other side. I stand up on my ladder and deliberately make no effort to attract a meeting. After a few minutes I am still alone and getting used to it.

A saved sinner

I attempt to cultivate the isolation. I smoke a roll-up and observe the Christian meeting from a distance. It's just boys – gangs of boys, shouting-on their teams. After fifteen minutes I am musing on the nature of the human species and how we are frittering away this unique opportunity to communicate with each other. This aloof observer status must have been the mind-set that gradually led St Paul to ostracise himself from the other speakers and finally stand in isolation quietly grumbling and justifying his position. What does he think he's doing now, after several years of grumpy comparative silence? I note with interest and then a little alarm that Paul is absent this week. Am I part of a bigger plan? Am I being groomed to fulfil his bizarre role?

I watch the antics of two scruffy young newcomers as they set up and climb two eight-foot ladders a meeting's distance apart. They must have had a bet with each other about who can get the biggest crowd, but they haven't reckoned on the terror of the opening few minutes. Once up and proven unsuccessful, they attempt an unrehearsed double-act to make light of their embarrassment – waving, calling and lobbing things at each other. Very soon they have backed down, abandoned their ladders and disappeared.

As I'm rolling another ciggie, I have my first customer of the day, Albert, who stands in silence beneath me, looking up with a daft smile on his face. He leaves, slightly puzzled and without comment when I say out of the corner of my mouth:

"Not now Albert, can't you see I'm busy?"

Paul would have been proud of me.

Hello Mum

Back at the pantomime set, a succession of people take it in turns to climb the two ladders: tourists and their children pose for photos, a drunk tries the ascent and ends up sprawling and finally it becomes a venue for bravado performance by local lags and frustrated speakers. The 'Hello Mum' novelty factor allows one or two them to make brief debut speeches, something they'd find almost impossible on a smaller ladder or a crate. I'm laughing to myself and wanting to share these observations, when on cue a small crowd gathers around me unsummoned and we start chatting.

The nonsense around the ladders and the mindless chanting of the religious nutters unconsciously imposes a serious agenda on the meeting. What develops is one of the most intense and longest meetings I've held so far this season.

There seems to be only one important news item that demands to be discussed, and that is child abuse and paedophilia. Hardly a subject I would have chosen for a two hour discussion by a bunch of men at Speakers Corner, but that's what happens.

What keeps the discussion hot is the diversity of opinion and the respect people are giving each other in return for their honesty. The presence of at least two separate strangers in the core group, both of whom are voicing right-wing opinions but who also appear to be lulled by the mood of a vague confessional, adds a strange air of expectation to the proceedings.

At first, it's all understandably a bit tentative, but I'm aware that several of them, me included, need to know that such a debate can take place – merely to justify our belief and continued patronage of the place as a serious forum for free speech.

People have been reading their papers and doing their homework. They are clued up about many aspects of the subject: abusers often being abused themselves, parental and sibling abuse being more common than 'outsider' abuse and other subtleties are all givens – although they have to be repeated periodically for the benefit of newcomers.

Pretty early on, I give my appraisal of the Dunblane massacre, which I find intriguing for the following reasons. Thomas Hamilton was a loner and seen as a weirdo by the community he lived in. He was most probably a paedophile who never acted on his sexual impulses. He nevertheless cultivated the company of children by working as a scoutmaster. But he was eventually sacked because he looked and seemed so unsavoury. He then started his own scout troop and organised camping holidays for young boys and was again stopped and denied further contact. There is no evidence that he ever abused a child; on the contrary his life was dedicated to them. But you could hardly blame the parents of Dunblane for censuring his activities. If ever he had abused a child they would have been culpable – the suspicion had always been there. He was slowly and understandably ostracised by the community until finally, a lonely miserable pariah deprived of any contact with their children, he took his revenge by depriving them also. He took a gun into the schoolhouse and massacred their kids, killing himself as well. The only points being: How do we prevent another Dunblane? And how do we treat the honourable abstaining paedophile?

After this contribution, I redefine my role, not overtly but in deed. I gently push the subject matter into taboo areas and let things take their course, acting as a chair and occasional contributor but not as the sole speaker.

I make no effort to build the size of the meeting by barking or encouraging those on the fringes to stay. I let the quality of what's being said speak for itself, consequently there's never more than 25 in attendance at any one time, and at one point it dwindles briefly to six.

Although women listen in from time to time the only contributions are from men. Neither is there any heckling, only discussion. Even Albert respects the vibe and returns from time to time throughout the afternoon without once interrupting.

The Appalling Lurch, with a few fans in tow, pays us a visit and spontaneously the meeting of a dozen goes silent, and remains silent for two long minutes until, frozen out, he leaves. We resume without mentioning him.

I try to guide the subject matter into how personal experience informs sexuality and, consequently, attitudes towards sexual politics. I don't push any of this directly, but again lead by example, offering insights into my own sexual experience.

There are periods of unease and shifting allegiances as well as a general male bonding. But I realise the camaraderie is fragile, so I refuse to exchange knowing glances with friends and allies and often I find myself holding back and serving only the debate.

There is little agreement on the actual subject matter. I personally am just glad that it's being aired. My only other main contribution comes when the subject is split into two areas – abuse of pre-pubescent children which, as you'd expect, is universally condemned, and the grey area of sex with consenting under-age adolescents. It's suggested that lowering the age of consent could mean decriminalising older partners of sexually active young teenagers. I am surprised at the considerable ignorance there is among some men of the tendency of many young women, including adolescent girls (sometimes as young as eleven and twelve), to seek the company and apparent safety of older men to flirt with and explore the power of their newly acquired sexual attraction.

I feel obliged later to repeat the details of this syndrome as a piece of public information, but not wanting to patronise anybody, I don't go as far as proposing a code of ethics.

It's the treatment and punishment regimes for offenders that cause the most arguments and the least satisfactory conclusions. Put them all in a prison-hospital on an island with a team of well-paid therapists is the nearest we come to a liberal consensus.

I confront those with the most rabid right-wing solutions by asking them how they would want to be treated if they had tendencies towards paedophilia.

Eventually the trust that has built up breaks down and an old-fashioned off-topic argument starts to develop between the libertarians and the reactionaries.

Interestingly, we wind up talking about fascism, nationalism and finally Englishness.

The after park pub drink becomes a regular feature following this meeting. Cheers!

Sunday 30th July 2000

There are no designated areas for religious meetings at Speakers' Corner, but today at 3.30pm the further west I heckle, the more I am going to burn in hell. I have a simple ploy to heckle Born Again Christians; it worked once and I'm staying with it. As soon as I hear the word 'sin', I want it explained. I improvise from there depending on how they deal with it. Twenty years ago I once had a grown man in tears when I asked him clearly, calmly and in a forgiving tone "Was it very bad? What you did?"

Moderate Islam

I regularly make the small effort to go right to the fringes and listen to Mohammed. He's a middle-aged black American Muslim preacher, professorial and dignified. He speaks in measured tones and thinks before he answers questions. He's easy to heckle, so I don't. Instead I just listen. I once listened to him have a formal discussion with the Christian in the suit, and after an hour of irreconcilable disagreement and mutual respect I walked away having learned more about the value of courtesy than the value of either Christianity or Islam. Today he is embroiled in an impenetrable debate with a group of young Arabs talking about stuff I don't understand. But I still give it five minutes.

Jesus Lives

Directly opposite I listen in on William. William is a hippie – gentle, softly spoken and at times apparently away with the fairies. I don't heckle him either. He's fifty-two, has long grey hair, wears bells, tie-dyed T-shirt and a poncho. A small group of foreign students are gathered round him teetering on the brink of community singing while he leads tapping his tambourine. He is just as likely to be found on the Portobello Road or at Glastonbury festival, and at first glance you might think he is selling late sixties/early seventies LPs. But it's only the covers that are spread out in front of him –

Santana, Pink Floyd, Incredible String Band; they are William's twelve-inch visual cue cards for his life's message. The music contains the spirit. The spirit unites the people. The spirit is the spirit of Jesus Christ. And William, prematurely frail and faltering William, is the reincarnation of Jesus Christ. It's true. Ask him. He'll tell you all about it.

Soldier Dave

I stroll back through the mainly religious meetings at the centre of Speakers' Corner to where Soldier Dave is attempting to whip up the masses.

"So when's the revolution starting then?" I heckle in passing.

"We've already started, you said."

"Just testing comrade."

Dave is a Hippie but joined a generation later than me and William. A man in his early forties who's been through the armed forces, done his

share of manual labour and has soft landed into an alternative lifestyle while he's still sane. Sometimes he can cut quite a dash in his freshly laundered white cotton suit, long black hair in a pony tail and zealous advocacy of a life of responsible leisure eschewing materialism. He talks convincingly of spreading love and resources around and backs up his words with actions. Dave's part of a little posse who bring free food and clothes to the Park each week. They distribute it among the street people who live on the fringes of Speakers' Corner in the various nooks and crannies of the Marble Arch traffic island. And of course to anybody else who wants it.

© Philip Wolmuth

William in 1978

Anti-Scientology campaign

I encounter a speaker now I haven't seen or heard before and who's definitely worth a mention. I watch him enter the park. A smart office worker type walking purposefully around with a crate. He soon finds a spot and immediately starts speaking. It's like this is his first time ever, and he's made his mind up to do it; and he's doing it. I stroll over intending to indulge him for a minute or two and end up giving him ten. I'm one of the first in his meeting, a few others arrive as I'm getting the first blast of his message. And has he got loads to say? He's a one-man campaign against Scientology – the twentieth century pseudo religion of L. Ron Hubard, which counts celebrities like John Travolta and Tom Hanks among its followers. Like new recruits with a new belief, ex-devotees can also get zealous about their new lack of belief. This guy's been right through the mill and believes his old spiritual masters are evil, and to prove it he's got reams of inside information he wants to spill. I welcome him, but to be honest I'd probably welcome someone from the Travolta camp as well. It's not really

Soldier Dave

my subject, but he's finding some willing listeners and when I leave him, he's explaining to a meeting of twenty the dubious ulterior motives underpinning the plots of L. Ron Hubard's science fiction stories. He's loving it. He'll be back.

Smile and say 'Jees'

Meanwhile there's a lot activity close by and I make my way to the front of it. A film crew, complete with technicians and people with clipboards (doing Jack shit), appear to be running a dummy shoot in the middle of the meetings. By the amount of talking into headsets that's going on, I assume there's a director sat in a van somewhere nearby giving orders. They are creating more resentment than interest, particularly when it becomes apparent that the police are complicit in their operation. No one is showing any overt aggression towards them but it's there under the surface. They're in our space and it feels as if they're about to do something tacky. Finally a plinth is produced and a gushy young actress/presenter type with dyed ginger hair appears, jumps up and starts shouting about sexual freedom; but she's not addressing the crowd – she's playing it straight to camera. They film her while backing away in a circle around her catching as much as they can of the bemused onlookers. Suddenly they get the 'word' to stop and they resume their starting positions. Yes! Now they're going for a take. We are being abused. I can't think what to do or say, it all seems so insular. The ginger woman jumps up again and repeats her lines, and round and round they go, reversing and forging a path through the crowd – there's a lot of pushing and shoving. A few seconds of this crass imposition and the voice of relative sanity arrives to disrupt it. A Born Again Christian – one of the compulsive ranters – jumps into the space created in the wake of the spiralling camera crew and bellows a repetitive mantra which drowns out everything.

"Jesus loves you! Jesus loves you! Jesus loves you!" He shouts raucous and monotonous, throwing his arms up to the heavens on each line.

They cease operations clearly under orders. This is met with a local cheer. They move to another position still in the thick of it, presumably their director thinks that he must have encroached on a speaking pitch. They quickly set up again checking light meters and sound levels. The Jesus freak, who hasn't really stopped chanting but just taken it down a few notches, has attached himself to them again and as soon as Ginger steps back on the plinth, he resumes full throttle. The whole sequence is repeated, only this time a neighbouring speaker, Dr Bulgaria – no mean resonant rasp of a voice himself – joins in causing laughter and more cheering by virtually everyone except the television crew, who are now really under pressure and are presumably being instructed to continue by their director who believes it can't last. But they haven't done their research. The power of the lord is everlasting and his minions have long-range yell by dates. They stop and they start. Several expensive minutes pass and the scruffy Jesus freak with the foghorn is undaunted and now being ironically urged on by a chorus of hecklers and spoilers up for a laugh. "Jesus loves you!" we all chant relentlessly until finally merging into a mass derisive "Ah!" And a celebratory cheer as the film crew gets the call to 'give up'. We have one final giggle – when all has subsided we hear J.C. Foghorn still chanting his message of salvation and still spiralling backwards thirty yards away on the grass.

In my dreams

It's only now that I feel inspired to speak.

"Jesus loves you!" I shout throwing my arms in the air. "Jesus loves you!"

I set up a short distance away opposite Martin who has his usual big crowd. I shout across to him. "Jesus loves you!" By way of salutation. A crowd gathers and they're in volatile mood. I try and start a discussion about the television crew, but the mood has been set and they are soon trivialising everything I say. Within five minutes it's noisy and out of control. Amid the banter and yadder of this verbal mayhem – with Albert wanting a dictionary definition of every third word I utter, Jeffrey heckling in a time warp and Adam offering me feed lines to some of my old jokes he wants to hear again – Andy the anthropologist says confidentially at my side: "Do you ever get recurring dreams about this place?"

"As it happens, no." I say. "I sorted all that out in the seventies. I just go flying in my dreams now."

He's interested. Of course he is. So I drop everything else and tell him about it one to one.

"My recurring dream is a flying dream – part of me is out there, every night in the early hours, flying high and free above the West London traffic. It wasn't always so simple. I put in some serious work a few years back – locating recurring dreams embedded since childhood. I learnt a bit about how to deconstruct them and take control. Point of information – When I was a kid, every weekend my parents would take me on the 607 red trolley bus from Hayes to Shepherds Bush to see my Gran. Did it for years.

Fast forward. By the early seventies, I'd screwed up my life something horrible. I'm unclear about the morality of anything I've done and I've run away to the circus, or to be specific, a street theatre group in Ladbroke Grove. I'd always had recurring dreams, but I never thought I could do anything about them. The most worrying and potent was the red bus dream. Always the same scenario – I'm downstairs on the 607 trolley bus, it's chocka and all the seats are taken. Among the passengers are the women in my life; they change from dream to dream. They are silent but they're giving me shit – ignoring me, revealing their pain and disapproval. I'm hanging about not saying anything and making it worse. Eventually I go upstairs. The top deck is empty, so I sit in the front seat and try and drive. I've got no steering wheel, no brakes, no nothing. Course I haven't. I'm upstairs. I'm out of control. The bus is skidding all over the road, people and vehicles are disappearing underneath out of my vision and I can't see what's happening to them. All I know is that I'm responsible and I'm feeling guilty about it. I wake up in a gloom."

I've got twenty people listening to me now and I'm on one.

"The theatre group starts doing dream workshops and everybody has to monitor their dreams for a week and identify their most important recurring dream. Then we act them out and deconstruct them. It's a long story, but I'll cut to the chase – how come I associate guilt with a red trolley bus?

"Well, whenever I was a 'right pain' as a kid. My Mum would go all exasperated and threaten me with "I'll put you in a home."

There's one or two murmurs of recognition at this from my over-fifties contemporaries.

"What she meant by 'a home' was an approved school. The only 'home' like this that I knew of, was St Christopher's School for Boys, but I never put the two together because no one, but no one, ever mentioned the place. It was there in our midst opposite the Bunch of Grapes on the corner of Coldharbour Lane and Uxbridge Road. But it was taboo to even acknowledge its existence. My mother for instance never said "I'll put you in St Christopher's." Because it didn't exist for her. She'd only ever threaten me with the cliché 'a home', an abstract concept.

St Christopher's was a tall redbrick building – Gothic Victorian – set in its own grounds with tall trees. If you ever caught a rare sight of the boys, they would always be wearing mustard-coloured shorts and jackets in heavy-duty corduroy, whatever the weather; inside or out, they would

Tony Allen under the plane trees

always be red-faced, at the double and under pressure. Strong imagery –
especially when you're pretending they don't exist. Now you know what it's
like waiting for a bus and it doesn't come, and how in the end you're almost
seeing it, but you're not. The Grapes Corner opposite St Christopher's, was
where we used to wait for the red trolley bus every Sunday."

"Ding! Ding! Any more fares please!"

"Shut up Albert! You don't know the half of it! And if I ever catch you in
one of my dreams. You're going straight out the window off the top deck."

Martin takes a break across the way and his crowd dissolves; suddenly
the size of my meeting trebles to seventy or eighty. A heckler plays to the
new gallery, but stays on-topic.

"I used to dream I was shagging the Queen Mother every night. What do
you reckon that symbolises?"

Another heckler replies. I don't hear it, but there's a big laugh. And now
the subject's changed to sex with mature women. I seriously truncate the
conversation with Andy

"Took five years of back street psychotherapy and radical feminism to
unravel that one. But eventually I got my shit together, went through guilt
and out the other side and, I kid you not, I learned to fly that trolley bus."

Now I try and grab hold of the meeting with an ironic: "One meeting
please comrades."

And I'm met with "Excuse me. When's the Speaker arriving?"

"Is this the homosexual meeting?"

And this, bless: "Were you aware that there's new evidence that
contradicts the previous orthodoxy that Rapid Eye Movement corresponds
to periods of deep sleep."

The superior man would see a challenge here and respond appropriately.
Me? I'd be quite happy to go down the pub with Andy right now and talk
about Polynesian communal dream flight over a pint, but then I notice that
a comedian mate – Ivor Dembina, who said he might turn up – is part of
the new influx. I feel obliged to crack a few jokes and put on a bit of a show
for him. I'm glad he turned up, in a way, because it's my perception of his
expectation that gives me fresh insight into what I am doing.

First time

The poet Allen Ginsberg had a dictum that an idea expressed for the 'first time' often has an elegance and purity of form that is elusive and difficult to recapture in the retelling or the process of writing down. Ginsberg, I assume, was referring to the muse touching a poet in the act of creation but, like many other live performers, he doubtless understood the artistic buzz and potential for 'first time' moments when improvising in front of a live audience.

Stand-up comedy, which is defined by its Now Agenda, can give the appearance of being wholly improvised. In reality, of course, very little is spontaneous and it is only the potential for spontaneity that exists. An honest stand-up comedian will admit that the moments of pure improvisation account for less than five per cent of their act.

When I was a stand-up, owning and performing the same routines to a different audience every night, that improvised five per cent of honing, heightening and embellishment became important for me – it kept me awake.

Lenny Bruce said that once his material became 'tight and polished' he got bored with it and discarded it. It was the lack of spontaneity that bored him.

What eventually made me such an inconsistent stand-up was that I couldn't hack the fundamental deceit involved in presenting only a semblance of spontaneity. Especially when I wasn't getting any myself. At Speakers' Corner it's impro central. I can be spontaneous all the time. All I have to do is be alert and up for it, and not prepare a set text.

For the next hour or so I spar around with regulars, speak to a large crowd and also take it down to a cosy chat with a few comrades, which can be overheard or not. Ivor's shock at the levels of audience participation reminds me of just how far away I am from stand-up comedy. This is the edge, the fractal boundary, and the cross-over between performance, play and real life.

Politics and performance

At Speakers' Corner the mode of performance and process of generating material is effected by two basic differences. First off, the front two rows of the audience are regulars and believe they are participating in something authentic, not watching a performance that only appears to be authentic. Also, everything I say has an ulterior motive. I'm involved in politics here, the exchange of ideas. Maybe I'm trying to prove, disprove, or illustrate something, but it's always a genuine two way process – I'm learning all the time and I deliver my arguments with borrowings and actual contributions from the floor. Familiar material inevitably becomes common property. The red bus story for instance, was a solo effort, fluent and authentic but only because it was the first time of telling. If it's ever used again it will be cited as an example of decoding a recurring dream. Much of it will be reduced to shorthand, put in inverted commas and, more importantly, other voices will be bunging in their two pen'orth and submitting minority reports. "Ding ding! Anymore fares please" may come very early on, may even be repeated. Fluency in public speaking, or the hybrid of public speaking that I'm attempting here, not only allows me opportunities for moments of 'first time' creativity it also offers it to the audience as well. My 'performance' comes from a wide choice of shared routines that might often only be references to routines and will always include a highly sophisticated level of audience participation. Horror of horrors for a stand-up comedian, I now consider it an achievement when the audience shout out the punchlines.

The politically hungry and homeless

I'm packing up to go when I notice that Nicholas' meeting, which has been going on for several hours, is now an intense leaderless discussion group of about twenty including several intellectual heavyweights.

Nicholas is a regular of many years and has previously not interested me because I'd associated him with a bunch of cynical hecklers, most of whom were white, higher-educated, right-wing, smart alecs. But in recent years he's been keeping different company and I've noticed him with his eighteen-inch diameter inflatable globe holding debates that have a quaint sub-public school flavour. Occasionally I've sidled up on his blind-side and listened in, and have been surprised by the content – radical reappraisals of world history and an understanding of the sorry state of the planet that is less motivated by eco-warrior concern and more by a hatred of his own class that have cynically abused their power.

I wheel my bike to the fringes and listen in. There is a mood of respect for one of the participants, who is now leaving. Bryan is very impressed. Apparently 'the guy really knew his economics' and everybody is thanking him, although no one knows who he is.

Despite their lively radical analysis, I have a problem with the pessimism of this disparate group of politicos. For me they represent a whole strata of post-leftist, whinging intellectuals who no longer believe in anything but have an avid appetite for conspiracy theories. They're going nowhere and doing nothing and they seem lost and defeated. They are the politically hungry and homeless. Some are ex-members of revolutionary groups, and in the eleven years since the Wall came down, and after three years of a Tory-lite Labour Government, all they seem capable of doing is shouting

© Ishmahil Blagrove

Nicholas

"Fix!" very articulately from the sidelines.

I'm not about to express this opinion, because I'm tired and so are they. But I do poke my nose in and suggest some lateral thinking, politely correcting their language.

I proffer 'money markets' instead of 'the Stock markets' "being as how 99.9% of the business done is the buying and selling of money at a mark-up." And later, 'the agri-pesti biz' as a substitute for 'farming and agriculture'. When the topic moves on to the oil companies and the multi-national car industry, I go into raconteur mode and give them a piece of stand-up material delivered as if spontaneous.

"I was cycling down the Marylebone Road the other day in the wrongly-named 'rush hour' and it was chocka! Wall to wall metal and carbon monoxide. I couldn't even get the bike through. And I'm standing there waiting for some give, when this bloke winds his window down and says to me, 'Can you see what's causing it?' And I looked at him and I say, 'Cars are what's causing it! Hundreds and hundreds of cars! Like the one you're in.' What did he think was causing it? A Serbian militia road block?"

I leave on this note, chuffed that I've made a good impression on the elders. As I cycle out of the park towards the pub I notice a familiar figure slumped in a deck chair.

"Well done!" I shout as I pass by. "You certainly sorted that film crew."

He smiles and then remembers his lines.

"Jesus loves you!" he croaks, hoarse and exhausted.

Sunday 6th August 2000

I arrive about 4pm. It's a sunny Summer's day and I'm wearing my new wraparound shades, which I believe might give me confidence in my mission for the day: to hold a sustained session of good old fashioned public speaking, rather than an intimate conversational meeting. I have to do this simply to prove to myself that I can do it. I've set myself some goals. I have to be thematically fluent and hold an audience of at least twenty for the duration. This means I've got to kick it out to the park all the time. No personal chats unless they are played for the greater interest. But first I have to find the courage to give St Paul my psychological analysis of his seeming inertia.

He has a smile on his face and a friendly word for me when I cycle up determined to gently confront him.

"I realise that this might be a projection of some of my own problems with speaking here, but take from it what you will. Are you really convinced that standing here, alone in contemplation, has any value? Are you still learning anything from doing it? Or is it just an excuse? Are you scared you can't speak anymore? Are you hiding from your own fear?"

He laughs, then smiles almost approvingly, but without giving much away. I leave him, knowing I've been cheeky, knowing I've been talking about myself, but also knowing I've been honest. I'm feeling pleased with myself and quietly confident. Even if Paul can no longer do it, I can still ride this monster and maybe even master the art. I'm eager to start, but opt first to take in some role models.

Listening to Ishmahil, I immediately get a fresh slant on him – he's getting a bit tired of his stock material. He rattles some of it off like he's a stand-up comedian with two more gigs to do later. He's much happier answering questions, and I notice that he's opting for improvised replies rather than something that he's bored with and we've all heard before. This is an advance and I want to watch more of it, but I'm drawn away from Ishmahil when I notice the Ghandi-like figure of Yusef speaking a hundred yards away. I don't often get the chance to hear him – our time zones don't mesh. Either that or he doesn't come down here as much as me.

En route I pass the anti-Scientology campaigner, who's debut appearance quite impressed me last week. This week he clutches a full-size purple inflatable alien. I listen for a few minutes while he explains another of L. Ron Hubard's bizarre sci-fi plots. He clearly gets off on this stuff somewhere because the irony is not immediately evident. To the casual browser he could come across as a weird advocate. It appears that in just two weeks he has joined the ranks of the loonies. Probably not a record.

Yusef

Yusef is about thirty, a slight figure in a traditional white Islamic robe, which on closer inspection looks like something he's borrowed from a hospital. His boney white face and frizzles of ginger hair peer from under a headscarf and give him a vague bird-like appearance. He stands on a stool

Yusef – the singer, not the song

surrounded by a large crowd, rather than backed against the railings. He speaks authoritatively about the history of Islam in a reedy voice with an educated accent with unlikely lapses into pure Trinidadian. Surprisingly, I find myself quickly drawn into following the debate due to his seamless recapping and awareness of the crowd's ebbing and flowing at the fringes. He gives cohesion and a sense of open inquiry to the meeting by asking various people, from all points of the compass, genuinely interested questions about their faith. Even the non-believers answer willingly, without fear of ridicule or intimidation. In front of me two be-robed teenage boys repeat in whispers any holy phrases he might utter. It all adds a timeless quality to the meeting. Yusef answers even the daffiest questions with grace and a lightness of touch rare among speakers here. He's a bit too earnest for my taste (I'm always hardest on my own faults seen in others) but he's decent, serious and from the respect he's getting from his elders, I assume well-read in his subject. He is clearly on a mission. He's wants to be a 'local guru'. I step back and do a slow 360-degree turn, counting thirty other speakers. In our own quirky way, don't we all? Thirty more like Yusef and it could be the new rock 'n roll.

I don't learn much about Islam from Yusef, but I do walk away from his meeting with purpose and some fresh ideas about attitude and subliminal crowd control.

I must admit that I'm finding the 'Advocate Heckling' far less important than the challenge of exploring the art of the speaker. I pick my spot against the railings under the trees, clean and replace my shades and half-face the sun and an imaginary crowd.

"Friends! Lovers! Comrades! Fellow creatures! Where are you?"

A small crowd gathers, including Kelvin who is becoming one of my regulars. I haven't fathomed him out yet at all – a sharp, Essex lad with an interest in the delinquent end of the arts. He's the ringleader of a little crew, who are always up to something curly. One week, they're dressed in drag and on E and enjoying themselves too much to participate; the next week they've started their own religion and are out recruiting among the dossers. After ten minutes of socialising banter I embark on a long stint very loosely themed around getting control of your own life. I intend to reduce any topical questions to their essence and discuss them in terms of my theme. I start off with a witty opening sequence that I believe captures a lot of what I'm about.

"Bigger cages! Longer chains! Better consolation prizes! Once more, with irony. Come on – all together now. Bigger cages! Longer chains! Better consolation prizes! What do we want?"

I laugh at the mumbled attempts to join in.

"We're in prison. All of us. We're in prison. Physical, intellectual, emotional, spiritual, prison. This is the weekly meeting of the escape committee."

"Physical prison? We're not physically in prison, now."

"Right on cue. Well done son!"

The heckler's a forty year old man, dressed only in shorts, a baseball cap and showing off his tattoos. Calling him 'son' gets a nice ironic laugh.

"Comrade, of course you're in prison. When was the last time you sat

Tony Allen getting emphatic under the plane trees

© Ishmahil Blagrove

around with your neighbours in the communal gardens, had a beer and barbie and then got into some serious mutual grooming?"

He laughs and so does everybody else and I carry on in this vein for at least ninety minutes. Sometimes I'm sustaining an audience of fifty, but it's usually around 25-30. It briefly falls off to a dozen on a couple of occasions when I wasn't so alert. But what the hell, I felt I'd accomplished what I'd set out to do and I enjoyed it. It also gave me a chance to recall and air some old routines and improvise some new ones – during the work ethic sequence, I slot in the gist of a forgotten comedy routine based around the phrase 'Good for jobs'. It starts from a rather pedantic contribution from the floor:

"Investment in depressed areas is the way to create jobs."

I often find it useful to repeat a question, especially when I need time to think of the answer. I also repeat the question when it's mumbled. Then everyone hears both the feed and my punchline.

"Investment in depressed areas is good for jobs? But then smashing your car up is good for jobs as well. Getting pissed, smashing your car up, hitting a few other cars, taking out a bus queue and ending up going through Marks and Spencer's window and requiring medical attention is also very good for jobs. Especially if you keep on doing it. Point being, what sort of jobs are actually necessary and what jobs are totally spurious? If some gangster in Sierra Leone, for instance, likes blowing people's heads off with a twelve bore shotgun and he wants to carry on doing it on a regular basis, but he's run out of bullets, and the government here makes some money available to set up a bullet factory in Barnsley – investment in a depressed area – then clearly blowing people's heads off in the third world is good for jobs in Barnsley. And by the same logic stopping them from doing it, must be bad for jobs in Barnsley. Discuss!"

I'm less encouraging of waffly contributions and engage with hecklers robustly to best them and shut them up. In retrospect, I was a bit insensitive and up me own arse at times and some of my regulars, who are used to making sustained contributions from my agenda, appear miffed when I cut them short and go for yet another sustained bout of ranting interspersed with rapid response heckler put-downs.

After I've finished, I get a few compliments and people asking me: "Why don't you do that more often?"

Towards the end of my stint, an earnest and very dull Arab speaker who I have seen for the last few weeks attempting to speak in broken English and only attracting piddling crowds, sets up close by me dressed in his best religious robes. Within minutes he is at the centre of a vast meeting of several hundred, speaking fluently in his native tongue and gesticulating heroically and to much acclaim. It lasts no more than fifteen minutes, when there is a prolonged round of applause and he steps down and it all dissolves.

A young Palestinian who occasionally argues with me, and has been watching, joins my meeting briefly, shaking his head in disapproval of the spectacle.

"The whole village turned out to see him."

He leaves before I can glean any more information. I'm not sure if the comment was a joke or for real. I put it to the meeting.

"What was all that about? Was it his birthday and the relatives were over? Will they all be back next year? Is it a cultural thing I've been missing out on? This place is so bizarre."

Nobody knows. Everyone seems to accept that the bizarre is common place at Speakers' Corner. I finish the meeting on this note. What happens next is equally rare and bizarre, but this time I understand it completely. Two visiting friends have just arrived and can't understand why so many people are attracted to such a bad speaker. They drag me round to witness something I never thought I'd see. Casey with an enormous crowd.

Casey has been a regular for as long as I can remember. Recently, I've noticed him turning up late, in the early evening when I'm ready for the pub. It's now about 7pm. He's not someone I would normally listen to other than for sociological and research purposes. He rarely stands on a crate or ladder but simply finds a space and rants and blusters his predictable Daily Mail take on the weeks news to no-one in particular for about twenty minutes and then disappears. His opinions are classic stereotype taxi driver. I join the hecklers at the back of the crowd, where I discover to my amusement and horror that it's true. Casey actually drives a black cab for a living. He must rehearse this simplistic garbage all through the week on unsuspecting punters from the driver's seat of his cab. A one-man operation reinforcing the myth of the right wing, loudmouthed, cabbie. He is very unpleasant – a gross-out. He froths at the mouth when excited, laughs at his own appallingly bad jokes and presents his offering as if it's a long awaited bulletin that people have been gathering to hear. There used to be a joke that he was the only Jewish member of the National Front. Somebody will tell me that's true, next.

Wrong time, wrong place – be there. For some reason or quirk of chaos, there are a lot of hecklers around, and they have descended upon Casey in force and appear to have been indulging him for some time. They are laughing at his jokes, or rather they are laughing at Casey as he is telling his jokes, which has inevitably attracted a growing crowd. Casey, who often bellows his thoughts out at full-volume to no audience at all, is encouraged

into believing that he has somehow got it right after thirty years of getting it wrong. It's late and a few speakers have also joined in before they leave – a spontaneous heckler's convention enjoying their one last act of irony for the day. The innocent Casey knows nothing of this and is now busy, trying to come to terms with celebrity. Up to two hundred have gathered and are listening. People have even sat on the tarmac in front of him, although not so close as to be in the saliva belt. Many of them are now beginning to see the joke; but not Casey.

A union of hecklers

Cynical James, an arch-heckler standing near me, asks a straight-faced question about street crime – a favourite Casey subject. He responds like a cartoon version of a Tory panellist on Question Time. Responsible yet rabid. Hilarious! This sport has been going on for some time – some of the culprits are holding on to each other, giggling uncontrollably. It's only when he's cheered back for a second encore, and the hapless turkey is starting to understand what's happening but not able to admit it to himself, that I start to feel a jot of sympathy. But he can't let it go; and once more he closes his meeting to ludicrous cheering only to return and pick it up yet again.

"Just one thing more I'd like to add before I go ..."

The joke is wearing very thin, and I leave for the pub with a bunch of thirsty hecklers bristling with a daft sense of achievement.

Sunday 13th August 2000

I arrive earlier than usual, about three o'clock and spend ten minutes with St Paul. I remind him of my question of last week. Vaguely quoting Jesus he tells me that what he is doing at Speakers' Corner is "Fishing for carp." And he adds, "There are so many minnows out there. I only want the carp."

He identifies with Jesus of course, and without irony. But he is still smiling.

Today I intend to make an effort with the Advocate Heckler role and also get some feedback on my current cyberspace obsessions, which will involve expressing some pretty complicated scenarios of which I'm none too clever on the detail. I'll be winging it some of the time and, as always, playing it by ear. Oh yes, I've also brought a couple of hundred flyers for a gig I'm promoting – the twenty-first anniversary of Alternative Cabaret at the Elgin on Thursday. I might even speak about that. I feel far more prepared than usual. First off, though, I have to warm up.

The Hyde Park Conservatives.

I join a large group of regulars including several speakers who are heckling a young Conservative stood on a dinky little six-inch plinth. They're having great fun at his expense. He's well-groomed, wears an open-neck shirt and slacks and exudes extreme normality. Humourless and earnest, he's like an on-message John Redwood without the personality. Several people are trying to argue with him. The banter is very Prime Minister's question time. I decide to be a surreal Betty Boothroyd and get my first laugh of the day with: "Will everybody please try and speak at the same time."

I'm stating the obvious because that's what everybody is doing, when they're not laughing. Tory-boy meanwhile is at the despatch box and in a brief lull in the merriment he's heard spouting:

"… Our record on education and the health service …"

His dogged belief in the relevance of what he is saying, and its stilted style, simply cracks everybody up. There is also a very pokey neat-weed spliff going round selected members of the crowd and it keeps coming back to me. Before I leave, I conduct a social experiment and stand blowing blow in his face. Findings: 100% of the Conservative Party speakers in Hyde Park are unfamiliar with the smell of cannabis. Bless.

I am feeling a tad guilty about the energy I'm giving to my promised role to the Arts Council of Advocate Heckler. Whenever I explain it to a crowd, they have enjoyed the idea, but so far this Summer I haven't actually done it. I'm not particularly worried about defrauding the Arts Council, especially when I am following a stronger artistic creative urge, but nevertheless a niggle remains and, honest soul that I am, I will have to make an effort.

I no longer have a problem about starting my meeting. And I'm mildly stoned by the time I get up on my ladder to speak and, with Tory-boy's style still in mind, I opt for an honest barking pitch.

"What must we talk about this week? What has happened in the last seven days that we need to discuss? You are here, in the so-called bastion of free speech. What shall we talk about? How shall we use the time? You choose. But know this, whatever subject matter you suggest, whatever questions you ask, I will use them to get on to my agenda, my obsessions, my own personal hobby horses. Know it."

This gets a laugh and the laugh doubles the audience. It is a joke of sorts, but a very local joke. I am describing what goes on in other meetings, and what will happen in my meeting. I'm honest. And already I have made a promise that I am going keep.

Questions from the floor

The first question concerns the continued daily bombing of Iraq by the British and Americans. I don't want to get bogged down with this; the questioner is a politico with an opinion to express. It's a regular hobby-horse topic in other meetings and already people are offering contributions. I decide to listen and put together a lateral answer. I develop my answer by confirming facts with the questioner.

"The evil Saddam is doubtless making efforts to defend Iraq against this bombing – maybe attempting to down a bomber, probably even moving larger anti-aircraft guns into the border areas where the bombers are most active. Yeah? Some day in the near future there will be some national scandal here in the UK, a major corruption, something will occur that we all of us need to know about, something the government would rather play down. Then, we will have front page headlines and news bulletins dominated by the evil Saddam pushing it to the brink again, and how Britain may be forced to go to war with Iraq. The Iraqis are already providing the evidence. It's a headline on the backburner. I just made that up. Plucked it out the air? Doesn't make it a bad idea. You believed it. I'm not very good at conspiracy. More of a SNAFU man myself."

I'm playing, and now I want to move on. I want to speak about the media and from there launch into cyberspace with the ramifications of merging computers, telephones and television.

Questions on the floor

Before this can happen, a drunk, who I don't recognise, stumbles through the crowd and falls at my feet. He stands up confused, leaving a bag on the ground containing two bottles; one of them is seriously leaking. When I ask him how he intends to get any drunker when his cider is dribbling all over the tarmac, he doesn't register what I'm saying, but assumes that because it got a laugh, it must have been a put-down. He consequently puts all his energy into heckling me and falls over again and into the puddle. I decide to put my 'cultural Babel cyberspace discourse' on hold for a while and instead discuss the comparative merits of cider and cannabis – his chosen drug and mine; but he leaves before I can start moralising.

Opposite, twenty yards away, Ishmahil stands up and barks probably his second session of the day. The interruption is over fairly quickly and he takes the volume down a few notches as soon as a crowd assembles. I resolve to go and heckle him at some point, but as an advocate on a mandate from a punter. This will involve coming clean about the funding I'm about to receive from the London Arts Board. It's another change of subject and I'd prefer to do it without too much disruptive heckling because, although I've written it up as a piece of prose, it's only just starting to take shape as a spoken word routine. I've entertained friends with it occasionally for a couple of months, but it's a long one and needs time and focus. I decide to come at it from a safe place and so steer the meeting on to the topic of the work ethic, where I can hold a sizeable crowd together, get into my stride, and then on to the 'your taxes pay for my benefit' riff. Then, from there it's a short step into Arts funding. I've no idea how many of them will stay with me till the end, and no sooner have I started than Cider Man returns pushing his way to the front to tell me with a slurred flourish:

"I'm going!" (Laughter). "But I'll be back!"

I decide to use him as a way of building Ishmahil into my other sub-plot and setting him up as a bit of a big deal with the crowd.

"So you're coming back are you? Now you make sure you remember me and where I am. I'm standing over there. That's me, see?" I point at Ishmahil. "I'm the big, cool-looking, black guy with the shades. Right. Right?"

He agrees.

"Okay, see you laters."

It was the last I saw of him.

Advocate heckler

I finally get to tell the Arts funding story. It's quite amusing and there's a crowd of about thirty still following the plot as I go into the background and fill out the details. I finally explain my role as an advocate heckler. On cue two young Muslim lads, in their late teens, who have been stood in the front rank of the meeting almost from the beginning, demand that I go and heckle Ishmahil. Ah, the power of suggestion. Point of info: They haven't told me they are Muslims but they've given me plenty of clues. Earlier, the more studious one has asked me what I thought of 'Jews'. I set the tone immediately by not replying with the old favourite 'I like all Jews – lime Jews, orange Jews, grapefruit Jews.' He knows I haven't taken this line when I reply.

"What all Jews? Or just some Jews like say f'rinstance Albert Einstein, Lenny Bruce and Bob Dylan?"

They haven't heard of any of them, so I bung in Chuck Berry for a laugh. But I digress …

"So what is it you want me to ask Ishmahil?"

"Why is he such a badass black dude."

"Sorry, I'm not asking him that! And anyway he isn't badass. He just puts that on. He's probably just a bit insecure."

There's laughter, but the lads don't laugh and they certainly don't believe it. If anything they're in awe of him. Perfect. Really what they want to know is 'whether or not he's a Muslim, and if not, what?' They are impressionable youth in search of a role model. The studious one pipes up again.

"Then ask him. 'What is his faith?'"

The other one agrees. This is really the question they want put to Ishmahil. I agree to heckle on their behalf and explain to everyone listening what is about to happen. A few minutes later I have found my way close to

Comparative religions

the front of Ishmahil's meeting. It's large and unusually quiet and relaxed; at least a dozen people are sat down at the front. The two lads, plus the rest of my meeting, are watching from the back. I listen for a few minutes, and then courteously interrupt.

"Ishmahil."

"Tony?"

"I'm here in my capacity as an advocate heckler ..."

Laughter including Ishmahil.

"... And I've got some people in my meeting that are under the impression that you're 'one badass dude'. But more importantly, they want to know 'What is your Faith?' What do you believe?"

Ishmahil

Ishmahil is slightly on his guard, unaware of what stunt I might be pulling. It won't be the first curve I've thrown him. For all he knows, I've got a camera crew in the crowd.

He seizes the opportunity to launch into a familiar (to me) riff about equality and people power. I'm delighted because I've got the perfect capper for all this sentimental pop-anthem politics. If only he'll give me the chance. He starts to dirty it up a bit – throwing in stuff about fighting oppression, and being against organised religion and Governments. He's a bit more lyrical than this, but you get the gist. He leaves me a natural pause. I spin round and address the crowd but particularly the two Muslim lads.

"There, see, I told you. He's just a big friendly pussy."

There is laughter. Ishmahil is no fool, and neither am I, so I leave while I'm ahead.

Back at my meeting the crowd reassembles and the two lads (being cool youf) are only begrudging in their acknowledgement of my work. Now they want me to intervene in the adjacent meeting in which Christians and Muslims are at it again staging their non-violent, but very noisy, re-enactment of the crusades. Things are seriously hotting up – a crowd of maybe three hundred with half a dozen police on the fringes are becoming deafening. I decline, and tell the lads that they've had their money's worth and must go and pay more taxes – do some work or consume and spend money – before I can act on their behalf again.

I shift my ladder five yards to the left, away from the noise, and embark, full of confidence, on the subject of cyberspace. I'm no longer concerned about holding a crowd together; I just want to get it all said, elicit some feedback and take in some contributions. On these terms I succeed and I do manage to maintain at least a modest crowd. I develop some nice sequences and surprise myself on how much I am learning and remembering. I'm quite pleased with myself – I've achieved more in one hour today than I have in the previous three weeks of speaking and heckling. Although, because of my sense of purpose, I have let a few hecklers off the hook – I've ignored them so they would go away. They in turn have been hit-and-run sniping on the edge of the meeting. Nothing disruptive, but they've been taking advantage. There are about three or four of these peripatetic spoilers present and I'm now ready for them. Okay, I know it's a male ting, but I've earned it. I indulge in ripping the shit out them for ten minutes. Ishmahil's crowd and my crowd are now converging in the middle. My ego swells in proportion to the size of the crowd, reminding me to transcend the cheap laugh and reveal the truth beyond. Oh yes. They don't call me Lofty Tone for nothing.

The studious Muslim lad is back and he's in heckling mode. He and his mate have been moving between the three meetings – Ishmahil, the Crusades and me. He asks me a question and I answer it with another question: "Why was the first question you asked me earlier about Jews?" But the truth is thwarted when his mate arrives and drags him away to the neighbours where the Christian/Muslim all-male synchronised chanting is building again and is now way beyond it's normal (unacceptable) decibel level. But fair enough, it's a big park. I decide to move and have one more go at cyberspace.

I return to my favourite spot under the plane trees at the junction with the main walkway and opposite Ali, who is in full surreal flight disturbing the minds of a crowd of fifty. The crowd that re-assembles in front of me includes the thinkers and regulars from just previously (a fair few carp) but also some fresh carp. I want to go back over the basics again to get every one up to speed with the subject. I express this dilemma to those who have already heard it and several of them volunteer to leave, saying they'll come back a bit later, which they do. I find this very touching.

So twenty of us go back to cyberspace. I'm getting hold of the subject now and have a beautiful moment when I prophesy 'a paradigm shift in the quality of intimate communication' and it actually feels that that's what's going on. I also get to slot in some stand-up bits:

"Direct communication, happening now! Full on, real life! Check the website at RL.com prefix http colon backslash backslash backslash stop it I like it www dot up yer modem round yer database and all for the price of a local call. I should coco! Have you seen my quarterly bill? Talk about telephone numbers!"

And a little later ...

"Perhaps you sit around with a bunch of mates, late at night, getting stoned out yer brains and having lots of wacky ideas. That's generally referred to as 'sitting around with a bunch of mates, late at night, getting stoned out yer brains and having lots of wacky ideas.' But, if you sit around with a bunch of mates, late at night, getting stoned out yer brains and having lots of wacky ideas, and you put all your ramblings up on website. That's an on-line thinktank dedicated to decoding the zeitgeist."

I hold it together for about half an hour with very few interruptions, and then Albert arrives and stands right up the front. What is unnerving about Albert today is that he doesn't say anything, he just stands there in near-silence, that jowly, bespectacled, dopey old face looking up at me with two alternating expressions – an uncomprehending wince and utter boredom pre-fixed with a deep sigh. No, Albert doesn't say anything, but I know that at any minute he will.

To compound things I notice Jeffrey the pedant out of the corner of my eye; he's another one of my regular awkward squad. Things are about to go seriously avocado so I decide to use Albert to explain 'cultural Babel'.

"Unlike the tower of Babel where everyone was speaking a different language, the Babel we are now entering is one of culture, of reference, of niche identity. With customised information and a myriad choice of available sources, we will all be speaking approximately the same language but we won't have a clue what is being said. Will we Albert?"

I'm expecting Albert to reply with the old favourite. 'I've just arrived can you start again from the beginning.' But he doesn't. He stays shtum. He's stuck in uncomprehending wince mode. Instead some youngster with his arm round his girlfriend, who has been listening for sometime, says, "What's a Babel?"

Someone answers him. "In the Bible – the tower of Babel ..."

"... Oh, this is all religious then is it?"

Then it starts.

"No, this is the homosexual meeting."

"When's the speaker arriving."

"I'm waiting for a number 12 bus to Queensway."

I didn't really need Albert, did I? Now it's me that sighs deeply and mugs utter boredom. I'm suddenly in minnow infested waters.

I don't remember much of the detail of the next twenty minutes except that Jeffrey refuses to understand that every day there are hundreds, maybe thousands of journalists submitting all manner of work which never sees the light. He doggedly maintains that in a scenario where there's millions of television channels and options to receive customised news to his own preferences, he would still rather watch "professionals like ITV." I finally lose my rag with him. Jeffrey's a dishevelled white South African in his late fifties, who finds change and new ideas difficult. For the last three weeks, he has managed to wind me up something horrible. That's not quite accurate – the problem is that Jeffrey pushes one of my buttons: he argues a lot like my mum. He'll say something very stupid, or rather he'll come out with some Daily Mailism that I consider very stupid – blatantly, embarrassingly, mind-wrenchingly stupid. And I will take the trouble to put him right, explain things, in step by step detail if need be, and check it through with him and everybody else. Then I'll carry on speaking again; and then, and it can be five minutes later, I'll hear "Yeah. But that's not to say ..."

"Arghhh!"

Thankfully violence doesn't come easy to me, but I'm certainly smelling its roots. More pertinently, I'm a performer, an artist; I would no more hit Jeffrey than I would hit my mother. I can own this stuff and find a way of expressing it. In an odd sort of way I s'pose I owe Jeffrey, not an apology, but a thank you, for reminding me of the psychological morass that is motivating me as a speaker and a person. No, of course I don't hit him. But I do leave my ladder and walk round screaming to the heavens and making a mildly entertaining exhibition of myself, very briefly flirting with the idea of setting up alongside St Paul and saying nothing for rest of the day. I probably enjoy the catharsis more than the on-lookers. One or two people, with genuine concern, encourage me to chill. I have a quiet moment and remind myself to ring my mother.

A little later there is a sudden crash and scuffle and an unlikely confrontation across the path – Ali is pursuing someone out of his meeting and they are now stood chin to chin in stand-off mode. I'm across there in a flash as a crowd gathers. For all his daft theatricality and surreal provocation, Ali is generally a calm and intelligent man and by the time I reach him, although still angry, he has had second thoughts and is backing off. I walk with him as he returns to his crate cursing himself for losing his rag. The police turn up.

"Ali. Take it easy man. You're not about to swear, are you? No? Good."

He thanks me and sits down, head in his hands. He's obviously over-reacted and regrets it. A cop comes over purposefully, but is very polite when he recognises Ali.

"It's alright. I know you."

A large crowd are milling about having been denied the spectacle of a fight. Several more police arrive, including a very attractive and obviously sexy WPC riding through the crowd astride a horse. She is wearing a tight shirt, tight trousers and boots laced up to the knees. Immediately the boys start expressing what most of us men are thinking and the mood quickly lightens, giving the police inspector a ludicrous dilemma. He elects to withdraw his troops and lose face.

I take advantage of the crowds and give out my fliers for the Alternative Cabaret gig. Kelvin is about to help but is suddenly reminded by one of his crew that it's ten to seven. He panics, rolls up his trouser leg to show me a tagging device on his ankle and shouts "Seven pm curfew!" His mates chortle and we watch him leg it out of the park. "What's he done to deserve that?" I enquire tentatively. Apparently he was dressed up in drag as a nurse and got busted for selling ecstasy at a rave in the West End. Course he was. Stupid question.

More advocate heckling

I have one last effort at holding a meeting. Martin's crowd next door is very lively and I shake my head snobbishly. Then I'm prompted to explain my theory of what is going on there. Earlier we've had a discussion about how to deal with crap behaviour from people who you know. And how, rather than whinge behind people's backs, it's important to call them on it and clear things up. Grant, one of Kelvin's saner oppos, points out that this is the second time the subject of Martin and his dodgy banter has come up in my meeting, and perhaps I should go and call him on it.

"Heckle him with it. Be my advocate heckler." Suggests someone else.

It starts to rain and the park empties, but Martin continues speaking. He has eighty to a hundred people clustered around him sheltering under umbrellas. I am bewildered at their loyalty and his sense of duty, or maybe it is just an example of the lengths people will go to hear someone talk dirty. With a handful of cronies tagging along, I make my way to the front and witness Martin teaching chat up lines to a group of young male foreign students. Along with the usual oddball chorus is a feisty group of young Asian women listening in, giggling and giving their opinions. I try and start a sensible discussion about the difference between love and lust, and although there are several present who welcome the deepening of the debate, we are clearly outnumbered by those who believe they are about to get laid or at least pair off and go for a romantic coffee. Warm rain starts to bucket down, and some of the girls yield to the elements – sing, laugh and clap their hands. I feel like a voyeuristic elder in the wet sari scene at the climax of a Bollywood movie. I decide to go down the pub and leave the young people to get on with it.

Sunday 20th August 2000

The eccentric, the exotic and Islam glam

St Paul has company when I arrive, so I'm prepared to cycle past him, but then he spots me and instantly proffers, "Think before you speak." And then, as I'm cycling off, he adds slowly "... And speak slowly."

It's surprising how little notice I take of him. For me, this weekly ritual has yet to be of any significance, beyond learning beginner's tips for speakers. I'm still having difficulty remembering what he's said, and sometimes it's only when I'm leaving the park and back on my bike again a few hours later, that I give him and his advice any consideration.

I park my bike near the Crusades, which are markedly quiet. A group of twenty or so Arab teenage lads, some in Islamic gowns but mostly in expensive Western suits, are listening to the Drill Sergeant as he compares the Bible to the Koran. They appear interested and amused and not at all moved to argue. More interestingly, there's a similar number of their female contemporaries, some of them extraordinarily glamorous and deliberately sexy. They are clearly wealthy and dressed in a style which flaunts their sexuality and appears to ridicule their religious costumes. Headscarves and even yashmaks are worn with naked shoulders and be-jewelled midriffs and there is a lot of purple about – purple make-up and purple accessories. Purple's very big somewhere in the Islamic world this summer. I talk to a few Arab regulars and one makes the rough guess that they are rich Afghan tourists based in Pakistan.

One reason for the strong Arab presence at Speakers' Corner is coincidental and due to the close proximity of the expensive hotels of Bayswater favoured by Arab tourists. The Edgware Road with it's Middle Eastern banks and alfresco Lebanese cafes serving black tobacco, smoked on the street in three foot hookah pipes, has an odd Kasbah-in-suburbia feel about it.

I've only ever heard about the Christian Cowboys, but I stumble on one of them next. Over a hundred people are gathered around watching three eccentrics. A bearded Jewish preacher in a sombre suit is ranting in Yiddish from the top rung of a six-foot ladder under the blue Star of David and steadying himself with the flagpole. A few yards away, an elderly be-robed Muslim cleric with an even longer beard is trying to get a word in edgeways from the floor. I can't follow the discussion and nor can anyone else because the Christian Cowboy, an Irish American dressed in a beige Prince of Wales check suit, riding boots and a Stetson, is conducting easily-led sections of the crowd in mass heckling. He sits on a crate between the protagonists and appears to be performing a crossover of semaphore and tai chi. On closer inspection he is deliberately misinterpreting their dialogue in mime – 'victory' 'no passeran' 'prayer' 'revenge' while also conducting a chorus of sound effects as the mood demands, which is every ten seconds. Ooo! Ah! Whooee! Boo! Hooray! Hiss! No! Yes!

A rollerblader enters the arena, does a couple of impressive pirouettes, gets a loud cheer and leaves, fist in the air. The Cowboy is encouraged to go one better and stands up to rabble-rouse the crowd further. I notice 'Jesus loves you' embroidered boldly in red up the seams of his trouser legs. Irish Chris appears in front of him and starts heckling. There are now at least four people speaking at once. I move on musing that I may disagree with what they are saying but I would die for their right to interrupt and heckle each other while they're saying it.

Frank, an East European radical who can see a conspiracy theory in a grain of sand, is stood with his bicycle chattering loudly with a few other garrulous headbangers. Close behind them, refusing to move his plinth, is the Tory-boy from last week attempting to project through them and over them to the passing crowds beyond. I don't see him at first; I only hear his wooden delivery spouting the clichés of current Tory policy.

It's here I meet the eccentric down-market dandy Tony Green, performance artist and creator of the bizarre Sir Gideon Vein character. He performed at our gig last week and promised he might show up to see what I'm doing here. He tells me that he's had a good look around and he's definitely having the day off; then offers me brandy from a silver hip flask. I set up my ladder, step up onto the bottom rung and loll there talking to him.

Immediately Jean, a bohemian regular who occasionally sits by my meeting reading or relaxing in the sun, asks if she can leave her bag underneath. She is followed by a bunch of anarchists who leave the bulk of their undistributed leaflets and magazines with me. Later, two other friends arrive and dump their jackets and leave us with half a spliff. My meeting becomes a base camp for people. I quite like this, but I'm less happy about taking messages.

"If you see my little brother tell 'im I'll meet them back here at …"

"No! You may not be aware of it, but I'm just about to change the world"

A group of 42 Kuwaitis (I count them) all holding placards written in Arabic, stand in a circle a few yards in front of me and start making speeches in a language I don't understand. They are technically in my space, if such a concept exists. After five minutes, I decide to bark a crowd and disturb them, but they suddenly chant briefly in unison and march off somewhere purposefully.

© Ishmahil Blagrove

The Christian Cowboy

I'm surrounded by about a dozen people, but none of them are waiting for me to speak, they are chatting to each other or checking in their baggage. I feel used. I step up and talk improvised nonsense for a while ...

"Lost luggage, tourist information, anarchist crèche. Leave all your stuff with me, I'll look after it. Directions given free here. Anyone want to know where to catch a number seven bus? Anybody want an argument? What's the capital of Bosnia? How many quarks in a proton? Who forgot to stop the First World War? What time's the ten o'clock news? How many eggs make seven?"

Then the drugs kick in, and I remember a subtle stunt to get my creative juices going. I start describing people as they pass, mixing flattery with occasional shafts of insight.

"Fifty vacancies exist for intelligent adults with good listening skills. Would suit studious looking tourist in khaki shorts and baseball hat, or youthful fifty year old male in second-hand Hawaiian shirt, or a mature woman in a fetching blue dress and moccasins. Audience auditions starting now! We're looking for bright pink faces with curly blonde hair and no make up. Couples that love each and are not afraid to show it by groping each other in public. Are you a scruffy yobbo advertising cheap brown sugar water on your T-shirt? Then we want you over here. Wanted three teenagers trying to look cool in baggy shorts and unfashionable tank tops. Are you friendly, attractive and dressed in passé faded denim? Ever thought about being an audience? Yes folks, if you're tall, black and built like Mike Tyson, then you qualify as a member of this audience. Dressed in a magenta top with unnecessary tinsel? Then you're perfect casting for the role of appreciative audience member for a loudmouth speaker."

I eventually get round to holding a fairly sensible meeting but I can't resist the odd description of passers-by and I continue doing it throughout the afternoon. At least ten people have attended the cabaret gig on the previous Thursday and I am now being heckled because I'm a fraud. No longer am I an anarchist layabout, but now I'm an entrepreneur. Huh! You organise one gig. The meeting continues to attract a contingent of hangers on who are just ligging around socialising, but they join in and support me when a group of antagonistic laddish hecklers pick on me.

After about an hour I decide to take a break and offer my ladder to Andrew, another ex-SPGB fellow traveller turned anarchist, who's got too much to say for himself. He prevaricates and offers to buy me a cup of tea first. Ten minutes later he's psyched himself up and is back and ready. I tell him he can speak for up to half an hour. He starts to talk about Big bloody Brother which, to my surprise, I find fascinating, but I don't put my two penn'orth in. Some ego trip stops me from being a heckler or contributor in my own meeting. I'm therefore easily distracted when I notice Yusef speaking.

Yusef is beginning to intrigue me and again I enjoy spending time in the comparative tranquillity of his meeting. This week he includes me in his arbitrary question and answer session and, when asked about my faith, I tell him publicly that I am still seeking. He nods approvingly and, although he is at least twenty years my junior, I temporarily regard myself as his spiritual subordinate. He involves me in further participation, asking those who have spoken out and anyone else (so anyone then) to find a few minutes to read the contents of a leaflet which explains Islam in simple terms, revealing it as a moderate and human-scale religion. Fifteen minutes later, I follow through at the end of the meeting and collect my leaflet. He hands it to me and, like a campaigning politician, he remembers my hook-line and comments.

"A Seeker eh? A Seeker is a good thing to be."

There's a film with Dirk Bogarde playing the black-clad atheist bad guy, and in the last scene he's dying and he allows the priest (played by James Mason), his old spiritual adversary, to read him the last rites. Dirk's last dying words are what I say to Yusef. "The singer not the song." He looks at me a bit puzzled but I walk away thinking I've been really clever.

Andrew is still holding things together at the drop-in centre and his platform has now changed to 'the therapeutic value of urban gardening'. He is slow to return the ladder and the eight punters. It reminds me of the stand-up comedy rule 'Never give a heckler the mic'.

Tony Green is chatting to a small group close by, but they join in when I take over again.

It takes me a while to get back into my stride but I finally pull a sizeable crowd, which tops fifty when I endeavour to explain (yet again) to Jeffrey my basic tenets of anarchy.

At first when he heckles me, I turn away from him and sigh deeply – giving it the full deflated body language – I let them see the energy drain out of me at the very sound of his voice; this gets a laugh. Then I mime an internal dialogue with myself and milk that for a few more laughs and I finally turn, mustering tolerance and compassion while muttering to myself in a stage whisper:

"Disturb the comfortable, comfort the disturbed."

I focus on him.

"So Jeffrey? Just how many Speakers have you turned barking mad today?"

Then aside and slightly paranoid:

"He might look like a harmless old scruff bag but I reckon it's a front. I reckon he's dangerous."

There are some regulars who do not find this local soap opera at all entertaining and they leave. I decide to go with it and continue the argument with Jeffrey and several other spoilers nit-picking over my two favourite paradoxes of anarchism. 'Property is liberty. Property is theft. Property is impossible' and 'There is only one rule – there are no rules. Therefore there are no rules against making rules. Organise only when appropriate.'

Jeffrey's inability to understand the philosophical efficacy of paradox and my seeming paranoia that he is in truth a mega-brain spoiler out to get me, leads me into a fine ironic performance ranging from extreme exasperation to composure and humility. I enjoy doing a running commentary to the crowd.

"See that. He's trying to lull me into a false sense of security by acting stupid."

Later on when I'm discussing clichés, a big bearded Geordie on a strong anti-feminist tip strides into the meeting to support me. He's failed to register the irony in my statement 'All women belong in the kitchen'. I recognise his mistake before he does, and string him along for a while and suggest he reads (and I make sure he memorises the title) *Goliath* by Beatrix Campbell.

There are decidedly more women in the meeting when the subject matter is about sex, relationships and gender roles and the more women in the meeting, the more men. I spend the final thirty minutes or so putting this rather obvious observation into practice, and find myself proving it true. There's an important lesson here but I can't help feeling it's a ploy on the same level as those gigs where they let nurses in free before ten o'clock.

Before I leave, I can't resist listening in on Born Again Diane. Diane is one of the most articulate and fearless speakers in the park, and certainly the most prominent female. She wears elegant well-cut fifties style clothes – neat suits and high heels which show off her trim figure. Her long grey hair is usually worn in a severe bun, and she speaks with an educated Irish accent. Often she has no plinth and stands courageously at the centre of a baying mob who rarely shake her resolve or her faith. Today she is in particularly severe mood (offsetting a bright blue summer frock) and has attracted her usual overwhelmingly male following that are heckling her mercilessly. She's under pressure and with absolute clarity she offers them her blistering critique of their wasted lives, particularly their obsession with

Born Again Diane

materialism and the sins of the flesh. As they giggle and heckle her, I take closer order and try and understand what is going on. She's on good form and for ten minutes I stand in their midst and attempt to support her, albeit with a touch of irony:

"Look at you! You lack pride. You're weak willed, you have no inner strength." She says.

"Good call. Be fair lads. Good call." I say in support.

"Each and every last one of you are strangers to spirituality."

"She's right again. This is insight we're getting here. Don't mock, listen."

Her analysis is not that far from mine or the SPGB or any other local moralist. Her conclusions however involve the wages of sin, Jesus Christ and the wrath of a vengeful God. She doesn't dwell on that side of things, much, preferring to hector and condemn, while dismissing what often appears to be the inappropriate sexual overtures of a bunch of very inappropriate suitors. I won't hazard any further analysis; I'm bound to get it wrong and offend someone.

The police knocking-off time seems at the discretion of the cop in charge. Today at 8.30pm, about half an hour before dusk, when tourist numbers are dwindling, a few officers go round gently hassling speakers and regulars to leave. There is no real pressure, and I'm standing watching Ali timing the end of his meeting with the end of a bottle of wine. A middle age cop joins the crowd and looks at his watch, and Ali responds by laughing as if to indicate that he's going to be speaking all night. The cop accepts the bluff with resignation and soon there are no navy blue uniforms on duty. This arbitrary laid-back arrangement actually undermines their whole operation at Speakers' Corner, because this is the time when things are at their most volatile. There are still dozens of groups, mostly in tight knots, surrounding and urging on nose-to-nose protagonists talking heatedly, often in their native tongues.

It's been a long day, and I find Tony Green and we go for a drink. Tony has enjoyed himself immensely, treating the experience like he treats life in general – like one long free festival – a fine role model.

Sunday 27th August 2000

Carnival

Today I'm not feeling on form; I woke up with a hangover after sharing a bottle of brandy with a mate last night. I live near All Saints Road at the epicentre of Notting Hill Carnival. Every night this week I've been in the street with hundreds of other locals, hanging out and dancing (demonstrably swaying) to the sounds of rehearsing steel bands playing popular classics. It's been exhilarating – like a community Carnival.

Today, tonight and all through tomorrow it's Carnival proper, which takes place on my doorstep. At midday when my neighbours start testing the sound systems and shaking the foundations of the house, I staggered out of my bed and cycled to Praed Street for breakfast. It's all too much for me. I usually go away for the weekend, but this year I'm staying. I feel a vague sympathy with the farmers in Pilton over Glastonbury weekend.

This visit to the park is by way of a few hours absence from perpetual gangster rap and urban festival. Quite a few familiar faces are absent, particularly the West Indians. I've arrived and set up fairly early and I'm telling my Carnival story to a meeting of thirty. Already, I've had an argument with some old grump who refused to believe that a steel band could play Tchaikovsky. I notice another Notting Hill resident taking a break, Lurch, but I don't have any sympathy with his position; he's part of an uptight residents committee who wants carnival relocated to Wormwood Scrubs. I just want one particular rig turned down a few notches and more portaloos, but I'm not complaining. Carnival has to happen, and it has to happen in the streets; that's the appropriate venue.

Millennium Dome

Talk of Carnival, Glastonbury, and festivals in general has got me on to a long-standing hobbyhorse – the Millennium Dome. I've had the same simple and insightful analysis of the Dome since the idea was first mooted a few years ago.

"Any creative promoter, who's ever put on an arts event or sports event anywhere, has got a fantasy squatting permanently on the backburner of their brain. They'd all love to do the perfect gig in a customised venue. But what sort of philistine builds the venue first, and then flounders about deciding what might happen in it?"

"Michael Heseltine!"

"Yeah good, Michael Heseltine. As soon as Heseltine suggested it, he should have been sacked. And he should have sacked whoever suggested it to him. In fact anybody who went along with it, should be sacked. And anybody with the authority to have sacked them and who didn't sack them, should be sacked. It's not too late. All of them should be sacked in retrospect. I'll go further, anybody who was offered a responsible job at the Dome and who didn't say 'Are you havin' a laugh or what?' should all be sacked. Especially all them advisers. Especially them, cos that's their job – advice. Not only should they be sacked, they should never work again. Michael Grade, David Putnam – all them philistine tossers! How much lottery money have they pissed away? It don't matter! The Glastonbury festival puts on, in one weekend, more creative art than the Dome could ever dream of; and Glastonbury gives money to charity every year. Any questions?"

I'm pulling a nice little crowd now and I'm back in question and answer mode with a subject I know I can go anywhere with – the definition of work and art. I have to keep reminding myself that this is the best modus operandi. All that John Wesley fantasy of talking for hours on end to an enraptured crowd hanging on my every word is not appropriate. The mixed ability shaman is a much better role model.

Anarchist initiation ceremony

An anarchist (black star in his lapel) looking cool in shades and a battered indigo leather jacket, who I met here a few weeks ago, is back again with a bunch of not-quite-so-cool younger comrades and a crate of cider. There's thunderstorms forecast so it's not really picnic weather but that's the atmosphere that's created as they pass me a bottle, sit down and make themselves comfortable. I decide to disturb them.

"Comfortable? I only ask because I'm committed to disturbing the comfortable and comforting the disturbed. Still comfortable?"

They laugh, which strengthens my resolve. I start off amusing them with some slogans and easy stuff – 'No rules' 'Property' and then I move on to stuff that might stretch them. 'There's never been a revolution without the police and army on side".

That worries them and they stand up again and start arguing with me. I soon realise that they are middle-class students playing at being anarchists for the summer holidays. One in particular, a bright lad with a plummy accent, has taken the bait. I go into a public one to one conversation with him and attempt to fuck with his brain for a while.

"Always look out for number one!" I say, pausing, long enough for it to elicit a negative reponse. Then I redeem it with:

"… Two, three, four, five, six, seven, eight … nine? Ten? Eleven? Anymore and it starts to sound like socialism."

My antennae pick up that some of the regulars are expressing familiarity with these routines. So I switch things around a bit to wrong-foot their expectations.

"There's only one rule in life. What is it?" I ask him and the meeting.

"There are no rules." Comes the reply.

"No, that's just politics. What about life? The only rule in life is 'Get in good company'. Don't ask me to elaborate. You know who's on your team. You know their strength. Do you know them? Love them? And trust them?"

I'm talking about my own recent experience now, but I don't admit to it. I've got myself into some bullshit guru mode, and the only thing I can do to temper it is parody myself a bit.

"So comrades, who are you and what are you fighting for? You are an independent autonomous group of what? Five? Six? Seven? More? You know, love and trust each other. What are you fighting for?"

"Anti-Capitalism" says bright and plummy.

"No." I say, ticking him off. "You can't fight *for* anti-capitalism."

I explain to the rest of crowd. "Anarchists have this problem with identity."

I'm treating the young anarcho posse as if they were a bunch of raw recruits. Which is roughly the case. There's real hostility coming off them now, and two of the four don't want to listen anymore, but they stay when I start speech-making and direct it to the swelling crowd.

"To define yourself in terms of what you're against is anti-dependence. 'Against the state! Against the police! Against the capitalists!' You are in an anti-dependent relationship with your enemy. They are in control. They do something – you oppose it. Wrong time! Wrong place! Be there! You might as well be totally dependent. They do something – you obey, you applaud, you buy and consume.

I take it back to the lads, "Independence is what we're fighting for."

I want them to smile. So I give them something daft as they are leaving

"So how many crews in a posse? How many posses in a tribe? How many tribes in a gathering? How many gatherings make a free summer festival?"

I get the feeling that 'indigo leather jacket', who is quietly smiling, is in some sort of mentoring role with these kids. There is more going on between him and them, than between me and them. They now want to leave and discuss things with him. There has been no collusion between us, but he's winking at me as if there has been. Whatever. I'm glad to have been of service. Although it would be fitting to pull a little stunt on him. He offers me another bottle of cider on leaving. I take one, failing to think of anything to give the kids a laugh at his expense. I smile and give him fair warning.

"You can't buy me off with your cheap champagne comrade. You're next! You've been warned."

"Cheers" he says, " maybe see you later at Carnival?" Which reminds me of the two Americans who agreed to "meet up in Europe."

"It'll be your first time then," I say. But he doesn't get the reference.

I drink the second bottle of cider as it if was water and it goes straight to my head and my groin, so I take a break and muse on the odd mythological fraternity that I belong to that exists among people who wear little black stars in their lapel or ear ring. It don't mean shit, although I would like it to … and that's where I could have got him, had it not been my taboo too.

Anti-evolutionist

Just as I'm about to start my second session, a couple of regulars, both atheists, make a larky request that I join them as an advocate heckler. They lead me to an articulate, educated Australian who, without any irony, is standing on an anti-evolutionist platform. He is convincingly sane, doesn't rant or ignore questions and argues like a thoughtful young college professor. In fact, apart from what he is saying, he behaves like a perfect gent. I suggest he must be doing this for a bet. Whether I'm right or wrong is irrelevant; it's not a bad approach. We assume he is doing it for a bet and attempt to have an in-joke giggle with him about it. Meanwhile doubt is sown in the meeting as to his motives, and that gets him rattled. After ten minutes, he looses his cool and it turns out he was mad after all or, to quote his best heckler:

"Everything is part of evolution. Everything. With the one exception – your brain."

When I start again, I never really get into my stride. The first thing I do is ask if anyone's got an aspirin. At least three people start heckling and calling me a hypocrite because of my slagging off of the drugs companies recently and how I said all our medicinal needs could be grown organically in the garden.

"Take a couple of organic tulips."

Acts of God

I should have packed up there and then, but Jeffrey has been heckling me, and two weeks ago I'd pleaded to the heavens to tell me what I'd done to deserve him in my meeting. Today, there's a storm brewing, the crowd is facing me and the trees, I face the park and the open sky. I could pull off such a ridiculous stunt if there was any lightning, which I'm far more likely to see before anyone else. I could then ask God to strike him down and wait for the thunder to crack.

Meanwhile opposite me, a bunch of clap-happy Christians who no-one's seen before sit in a little circle and start singing. They're not really bothering anybody, although they are quite near to Turncoat Toby who decides to one-up them and move in front of them and launch into an anti-religious tirade. They in turn start singing like there's no tomorrow, which is their thing anyway. A crowd gathers and most of my meeting go and join in. I stay where I am and amuse myself by shouting out daft things from a distance:

"Don't forget comrades – those without compassion will be shot."

Eventually the police arrive and inevitably see Toby as the villain of the piece. That is until a few regulars including Nick, Toby's old comrade in the SPGB, start heckling the Christians in front of the police. 'Upping the ante' is the house style at Speakers' Corner. Others start to join in, but the blossoming of a little local chaos is nipped very quickly in the bud by an astute move from the constabulary. Very quickly it is deemed that the playing of a musical instrument – in this case a guitar – is against the Hyde Park by-laws. The police make them put the guitar away and carry on unaccompanied. Normal service is resumed.

Half an hour later it rains, but I don't see it coming. Jeffrey avoids the wrath of God and we all get a short, sharp soaking.

Sunday 3rd September 2000

This is the first Sunday of my Year of the Artist residency. I treat it like any other, with one exception – this week I display my board:

TONY ALLEN

AVOCATE HECKLER

ANARCHIST PARASITE

MIXED ABILITY SHAMAN

newagenda.org.uk

White lettering on a black background with a modest motif around the border – a commissioned work by Georgia Wisbey, artist and sign writer.

For research purposes, I've actually been in residence almost every Sunday throughout the summer experimenting with ways of speaking and heckling. It's what I've done sporadically for many years, but this 'artist in residency' tip has encouraged me to concentrate on the different aspects and explore them. After three months, I've become less interested in the advocate heckler role and got far more excited by the artistic possibilities of deconstructing public speaking from within. My mission now is to expose by example the manipulative power of the charismatic orator. By way of back up documentation I'm also producing this journal written up from my diary notes.

I've been honest with the locals and explained publicly what I am doing. As far they're concerned it's business as usual, and if I've managed to wangle £300 a week for six weeks off the London Arts Board, then good luck to me. This funding scam has not been without its downside …

Will it affect my benefit?

After several unsuccessful interviews with Job Seekers Allowance officers, I've had the hassle of signing off the JSA. This snowballs into: I also have to close my claim for housing benefit; inform the local authority that I am now liable for council tax and respond to their forms, which are almost as ridiculous as the Arts Council's; reorganise the standing order for my rent; have a dental check up while I'm still receiving benefit; re-negotiate the terms of two debt repayment schemes; inform the Inland Revenue, to whom I also owe money and legally have first shout at any earnings. This is before I even start on the morass of becoming self-employed, including taking out public liability insurance and finding out how and where I pay National Insurance contributions. Endless phone calls – 'you are held in a queue, your call is important to us, meanwhile here's yet another five bars of Mantovani'. Aargh! Phone calls, interviews and forms. Hang on. I'm a creative artist. I'm on a mission. I've got a 60,000-word journal to write! And that's not the half of it. In six weeks time, I'm going to have go through the far more horrendous experience of signing back on again, then I'll see some fucking forms! And they wonder why people get into benefit fraud and victimless crime. Hel-lo?

At 3pm, I arrive via the sunken precinct on the Marble Arch traffic island, a stark paved area where people sell pamphlets, beg, busk and congregate outside the public toilets. Soldier Dave and Free Market Kurt are giving away food to the hungry and homeless and to anyone else who wants it. It's mostly sandwiches and rolls wrapped in cellophane that by Monday will have passed their Sunday sell by date. Kurt goes round collecting these from shops in the Edgware Road the previous evening. They're not part of a welfare organisation; they just do it. This week Dave has also come by hundreds of brand new CDs, and he's distributing them too. Tourists have joined in, rubbing shoulders with the dossers, browsing what's on offer.

A few minutes later, I surface and I'm approaching St Paul determined to remember his thought for the day, and also try and get a handle on why I invariably forget it. Paul, however, is in deep conversation with a young woman, so I don't interrupt. They really are on one, probably talking more sense than the rest of the Park put together. So I cycle past, and he acknowledges me with an appreciative nod.

Ali, always the committed surrealist, has draped himself in the flag of St George this week and is holding a cauliflower, a pumpkin and a very lively meeting, which includes several regulars. I park my bike in the usual place behind him and then set up my ladder, with its new board, close to where I intend to speak. Alan the litter picker reads the text aloud and this attracts some interest and amusement. I share a spliff, socialise and then go off to heckle, happy to leave my belongings over-looked and safe.

I'm becoming much more wary about the type and amount of dope I'm smoking when I speak and, without going into too much detail, this stuff today – in extreme moderation – is perfect. This is confirmed as I relax into some fluent banter with a smartly dressed Born Again Christian I've not encountered before. I'm honest with him about my belief in the importance of spirituality and how I am still seeking it in my own life. My openness encourages the poor sod to reveal that he works in a call centre with eighty others, each isolated in a little cubicle with a phone, computer and a set text designed to persuade small businesses to change their insurance arrangements. "And now" I point out, "you're doing much the same thing on your day of rest." I deliver this not as a punchline to get a laugh from the little crowd that's gathered, but more as a sympathetic observation from a Christ-like well-wisher.

I leave him with that and go and watch Ishmahil, who is having a head to head debate with a Muslim grey beard. They are stood on high ladders six feet apart in front of a crowd of two hundred, the main constituency of which is young Arabs. Ishmahil is respectful but still going for the laughs. Standing at the back of the meeting I can't hear everything the old boy is saying, only Ishmahil's reply, so I shout, "Repeat the question." Ishmahil does so with the next question, but I now feel as if I've over-contributed. I mean, who am I to start on-site coaching of one of the most successful crowd-pullers in the park? Best go and start my own meeting.

I no longer have any of that 'stepping into the abyss' anxiety about the first few minutes up the ladder. I now look forward to it. Although I do start off with a mild rejection – a classic stereotype bedraggled dosser walks up to me and reads my board without acknowledging my existence. I try and catch his eye but he's in his own drab little world. Everything about him, his long hair and beard, his clothes, his boots, even his mood are a monotone muddy grey colour. Everything, that is, apart from the bright yellow and blue cover of an Aretha Franklin Sings Gospel CD he clutches in his hand. He shakes his head in bewilderment and scuffs away. More people gather round and I am soon explaining the concept of 'Advocate Heckler'. Alan says the one speaker he'd like to see seriously heckled is me. He's the first of many who want me to heckle myself. I tell the meeting that I'm regretting the fact that I've presented every would-be comedian in the park with an obvious gag, but luckily Albert arrives unawares and triumphantly bleats out his version of the same and is met with a chorus of groans from the regulars. That's one job delegated. Albert likes the idea of the board. As I speak, I notice him deliberately puzzling over the text. It'll give him the opportunity to interrupt and query quirks of my vocabulary anytime he likes. Usually he has to listen and wait before he can pick me up on something I've said, but now I'm giving it to him in black and white, and he doesn't even have to pay attention. Sure enough, no sooner have I got into a riff than he chimes in with, "What's a shaman?" One of his fellow trivialisers informs him that it's like a she-man only spelt differently. I grab hold of the situation before it deteriorates and perform my explanation theatrically to the crowd that's now building.

"A shaman's job is to take lots of drugs, indulge in all the pleasures available and then meditate and ponder obsessively on all the shit that's going down for members of the tribe."

"You'd do that for me?" Asks Albert.

"I would," I say.

"… And then, he has to take some more drugs, get himself into a trance-like state, and appear at a pre-ordained gathering of the tribe …" I gesture to the here and now.

"… And then, finally, when everybody's in a receptive mood and ready to hear some truth, he *catharts* it! All over them."

Albert adds to the laughter by staggering backwards into the crowd. I vaguely recognise the faces of a couple of black-clad anarchists – probably come to check me out. I decide to give them a show, so I get back on to my original theme, and launch into a highly subjective explanation of arts funding, associated benefit hassles, and the larky scam details of my two applications. It's a long one, people are very interested; they're listening and they're laughing. Even the hecklers have shut up.

I describe staying with a community of socially excluded eco-warrior artists who have occupied a derelict farm in Kent. I am aware that it's a subject that most of them only ever perceive in media clichés and now they are getting some first-hand information. More to the point, I'm reminding them of their own fantasies and causing them to reflect on their own lifestyles. This is a lot of stuff to be thinking in split second blips while my train of thought serves the telling of an anecdote. I could get derailed here. I could lose my timing. Shit! I could literally lose the plot. Just in time I express what I'm thinking.

"You've all got your own versions of this fantasy sitting somewhere in your heads. How do you make it reality? How do you gatecrash your own fantasy?"

There's now a crowd of about a hundred hanging on to my every word. I try and keep it authentic but I've started sloganising. Anything could happen.

"We all of us live in prisons – physical, intellectual, emotional and spiritual prisons. This is the weekly meeting of the escape committee."

Sometimes when I come out with this sort of stuff, I give it arrogance and it sucks – it all comes across as if I'm trying to guilt-trip people into considering anarchist ideas. Which of course I am. It's all pure projection and it shows, but that doesn't seem to stop me. I usually get it wrong, but this time the tone of it feels right, because I also manage to express what I'm thinking.

"You don't need some loudmouth in the park to tell you about personal freedom. You know better than me what it is that shackles your creativity. You know what's stopping you. Duty? Commitment? Work? Mortgage? Relationship? Family? Something good on the telly?"

They don't laugh; they listen. It registers with me. I've got them! I'm giving them something they didn't know they wanted. I'm doing the business – the artist as opposed to the entertainer. Sweet as a nut, man. 'Sweetaz! You're having a moment.' Whoops! That's all I need – my ego sitting shamelessly on my shoulder, patting me on the back and whispering compliments in my ear. 'A moment! You're having a moment. You know it and they know it! Sweetaz!' I'm alert. I have to express this stuff and have done with it. Again – address the now! I pause, briefly looking round the crowd acknowledging the extraordinary focus I've got. Without moving a muscle, I smile to myself and say impishly.

"Carries on like this Albert, we could be having a 'shamanic' moment."

It gets a quiet appreciative laugh from a section of the crowd. Probably unacknowledged by most, just a passing laugh line, but for me it is a shamanic moment and I want more. I've started off right, and now I'm flying. I elegantly segue back to the plot and now include myself.

"I know what it is that stands in my way – me! I'm my biggest problem. I'm a slob! I've got some really bad habits. Freedom is a full time career. I have to be always vigilant, otherwise my life can slip into some very slack ritual. Sometimes, I need a jumbo crowbar to get me out from in front of that telly. I mean, how much daytime television can one layabout watch?

"Or conversely, when I've made the effort and spent a day or two on the phone getting a crew together organising and delegating stage, lights and sound; when I've booked the acts and I'm there on-site, having gatecrashed my own fantasy – a sort of New Age Humphrey Bogart in Casablanca – I'm sat round that campfire with a bunch of wacky mates, experiencing an all-day-all-night, post-mod, acoustic, cabaret party, I don't want to be anywhere else. But they are the only options people. Slobbing out or getting it on. And getting it on is only a creative version of slobbing out. It ain't difficult."

It is difficult. Of course it is, and I know it. Nobody heckles or says anything so I force them in to it.

"We can't be wasting our time doing anything else, can we? We certainly can't be wasting our lives 'working for the Man', can we?"

"It's alright for some."

"Yeah. You're being paid to be an anarchist layabout."

At last, they're heckling. For a moment there, I thought I was being too charismatic for my own good. I incorporate one of my regulars into the proceedings – Adam, who's a psychiatric care worker. I explain that Adam has a very important job.

"When you lot have been working so much that you're all worked out. And you finally snap and crack up from the alienation of it, it's Adam here what picks up the pieces. Adam deals with people with stress-related illness due to work.

"But now, Adam is off sick. He's got to have three months rest because he's started cracking up too. He's sick. He's sick of working with people who are sick of working. So stop work now! If only to help the Adams of this world."

They're a very mixed lot, this crowd, and I've woken them up – touched a few nerves. People argue when they are on the defensive and the heckles come fast and furious. I get indulgent – guilt trip them. Blame them. Don't let them off the hook. Then I rub their faces in it. I thank them for paying their taxes so that I can live a life of ease. There is a peculiar consensus – it is acceptable for me to be receiving money from the Arts Council but not from the Social Security, even if it is five times as much. I decide to push it. Over the weeks, I've done little to dispel the popular myths about arts funding and I repeat them again now – most of the tax-payers hard-earned money goes to the Dome, the opera and suchlike, which I condemn as outrageous, especially when compared to the piddling amounts given to the important stuff like homosexual theatre groups standing around naked and swearing at small audiences, sculptors building erect penis's out of elephant dung, unmade beds, sheep in formaldehyde, and face-painting in children's homes. In fact I'm happily reinforcing all the tabloid stuff and adding a few spurious examples of my own. My devil's advocate position is: not only must artists be allowed to experiment, they must be forced to experiment. If artists don't experiment they should have their grants cut. The only problem I have with the system is the jungles of bureaucracy artists have to deal with before they can put dung to armature.

It's beginning to register with me that there's a lot of other speakers in the meeting – Bryan Z, Heiko, Nicolas the Globe. Twenty or more people are sat on the tarmac at the front, and they're standing five or six deep beyond that. On the side by the railings, Turncoat Toby and Guru Barry have brought seats with them. On the other side, the fringes of the crowd have spread across the walkway to the edge of a smaller meeting. 'I'm blocking the road! Oo! I am doing well.' It's the ego agenda on my shoulder again. I address the now! "If you're going to stand and listen to me, can you make sure that you block the path and interfere with the other meetings. Thank you."

But I didn't express it all. My ego is still grooving on the size of the meeting and the presence of the local luminaries. How long have they been here? You never know with speakers; unless they are having a warm-up heckle, they tend to creep up on each other. Did they catch my shamanic moment? Whatever! They are now witnessing me losing it. I'm not paying attention. I'm getting angry with the smart-alecs. I'm definitely losing it. I'm not paying attention. The adjacent meeting has stopped because of the size of my crowd. Well clever me! But I'm not paying attention. I've just told a heckler to shut the fuck up! It gets a laugh. But then some people will laugh at anything. I'm not paying attention! The subject matter has shifted to 'property' and I haven't really noticed because I'm not paying attention. An aggressive young estate agent is scoring points off me and I'm just calling him names. Lateral thinking fails me. I hear myself call him "a greedy little arsehole!" Which he is, but it hardly adds a new dimension to the argument. Yes, I'm losing it. Going, going, gone! I don't remind the audience that the biggest chunk of almost everybody's budget, the thing that gives most people the most grief, is their rent or mortgage and this greedy little arsehole and the system he works for is getting a fat rake-off from our misery. No I can't think of anything along those lines. I won't think of anything like that until I experience an esprit d'escalier four days later in Queensway.

Now, I'm struggling to string a sentence together. Luckily the estate agent has made a few enemies in the crowd and has his own hecklers to deal with. No thanks to me he's screwing up big time. I tend to forget how unprepared hecklers can be. He's immediately on the back foot with nowhere to go and comes out with the first piece of bigotry he can think of, including a load of racist abuse apropos of nothing. He's not attacking blacks *per se*, he's attacking our liberal sensibilities. But I don't collect that thought at all. The tapes that are running in my head are all spilling from their spools, and I'm chugging along on a below average default. I tell him to go and tell Ishmahil or Ali what he thinks of black people. When I hear myself say this, I am appalled with myself. I stop and take a swig of water. As I lean my head back and look up into the foliage of the plane trees above, I reappraise my drugs regime. I vow to get a grip. Red Nick says something encouraging close by and we exchange glances. He's seen me on better form than this, and less than twenty minutes ago. The young arsehole has annoyed a few people, including the two anarchists. He doesn't know whether to leave or have a tanti, so he does both. Dragging a girlfriend behind him, both of them leave screaming and shouting out what sound like Alf Garnett impressions. Bizarre. He was so coherent to start with.

Then a woman's voice rings out loud and clear straight from an assertiveness training workshop ...

"What I would like to know is ... in this anarchist society that you are advocating, how do you propose to organise the maintenance of the sewers."

There's a few groans from regulars. Somebody laughs at the groans. I've got several answers to this one; it's a perennial. Is someone having a joke? This is underarm bowling. Someone's patronising me.

"Who does the dirty jobs that no one else wants to do?" She continues.

I find her in the crowd – a middle-aged suit with dyed red hair. She means it and she wants an answer. There'll be those in the crowd that were thinking the same thing, and they'll be wanting an answer too. There'll be some in the crowd that think she's really bright for thinking of it 'Doh! Oh yeah. Who does the dirty jobs.' I look at her and sigh. I can't be bothered. I patronise her.

"Don't worry about it. You won't have to. I'll have a word, straight after the revolution. You can be exempt. Anyways, we'll need your business and management skills elsewhere."

"Don't presume things about me that you don't know. I'm not in business or management."

This gets a mild "Wooe" from regulars. But she's back in the debating chamber.

"You still haven't answered my question. How do you propose to organise the maintenance of the sewers?"

I don't say anything. I'm bored with 'the sewers'. Somebody else can answer her. I want to say something I haven't said before. I want to surprise myself and everybody else. So just for the devilment of it, I ask if there are any volunteers to do the sewers after the revolution? None of the boring bastards says anything. I'm actually pissed off with them. Where's their sense of humour? It's not as if it's a binding contract. But I don't give voice to any of this, instead I moan:

"Someone volunteer. It'll shut her up."

"So much for the anarchist revolution" she says, and leaves triumphantly.

Another satisfied customer? Hardly. All this has confused a lot of people. Me included. What I think happens in these situations is that I can't bear to go through the motions of repeating myself – doing old material. So I wing it instead, hoping the muse will touch me, and when it doesn't, a little cloud drifts over me and sometimes I lose the will to live. That's where I am now. John Connor, a journo on the now defunct City Limits listings magazine, once told me that I'd be quite a good stand-up comedian if only I didn't keep shooting myself in the foot. But then, what does he know about it?

I'm not paying attention again. There's a bit of shuffling as people leave and others move forward. A scruffy bohemian in a white suit and cravat joins Guru Barry and starts chatting.

"Any Questions?" I ask, and to my surprise, it focuses things immediately.

"What anarchist persuasion are you?" asks White Suit.

This is a subject I've parodied over the years. If I choose to, I have a whole routine I can pull out of the archive, which trips off my tongue and finishes with "... I'm not yer bombs and barricades, small minority of troublemakers intent on violence in an otherwise peaceful demonstration style of anarchist. No. But then neither am I a fluffy CND pacifist. I'm more yer sort of 'naughty tendency'. Thirty years I've been an anarchist – naughty tendency."

But for some reason it eludes me and I don't go down that route. After three months of trying, I am finally realising my fantasy. I'm holding court in front of a very big (if dwindling) crowd on a beautiful sunny afternoon in the park. I'm gently stoned; someone has just asked me a question that I've got an entertaining answer to. And how do I respond? By painting a bullseye on my chukka boot.

"I don't know what you're talking about" I say.

And then I get all grumpy and start arguing about how he wants to put labels on me. I tell him that I'm an individual. He suggests I'm a follower of Max Stirner. I wish I hadn't heard of Max Stirner and get ratty with him, accusing him of being an 'anarcho-trainspotter'. The meeting has halved. This is ridiculous. This is the public speaking equivalent of suicide. And I've been here before as a stand up comedian. What is it with me? Is success so bad? There's a syndrome and I think it applies. I don't believe I deserve to succeed.

As quickly as the mood descended, it lifts. I relax and start to pay attention. Nicolas the Globe asks a question in a tone of voice straight out of a quiz show. "What is the significance of the black flag?"

I repeat the question. Not because it wasn't heard (he's louder and clearer than I could ever be) or because I'm giving myself time to think. No, it's because I feel extraordinarily fragile and I'm trying to get a grip. I'm monitoring myself. I'm unsure what I will do.

"The black flag means – no flag; no country; no nation; no master's ensign or maker's brand."

Is the correct answer, and succinctly put. I start to work the crowd and within a few minutes the numbers are growing and so is my confidence. I'm back up there again having more moments, finding the lateral, addressing the now and delighting in being alive.

"Do you ever doubt your beliefs?" asks a young lad sat up the front.

"Doubt? Yeah man, course I have doubt. That's why I come down here and shout me mouth off about it. See how it sounds in front of you lot. Doubt. That's why all these speakers come down here. Do you think any of these ranting messiahs have found the meaning of life? Course not. Check 'em out. Most of them are in pain. Most of them need a big hug."

My renaissance lasts for half an hour and then I chose to close the meeting when there's still a big crowd. At last I'm learning the local machismo.

What follows clearly goes with the territory. I'm off the ladder and clearly taking a break, but nevertheless an arbitrary queue has formed. Apparently I'm available for one-to-one consultations. I embark on a series of conversations with people who treat me like a priest-cum-therapist, culminating in a destitute thirty year old bloke from Newcastle whose marriage has fallen apart because of his obvious drinking problem. He pours his heart out to me. Every time I have a halfway decent session I become a very particular type of public property. These encounters aren't just people coming up after a gig and saying 'Wicked lyrics man, cheers'. This is people seeking serious help, spiritual sustenance and even leadership and I don't do any of them things. Maybe I come across like a father figure, I'm not of course – check my record – I'm more of a dodgy uncle. I'm an irresponsible artist, doesn't make me a bad person, just an inappropriate care worker.

My friend Jimini Moonlight, who's over from Amsterdam, arrives in the middle of one of these consultations. We'd planned to meet here at 6pm and she's very early. She says she wants to look round on her own and will be back in forty-five minutes.

I'm up for a second speaking session. It would nice to pull it all together again and have another big meeting and a few more moments, and of course show off to my mate.

I bark a crowd with the legend "Compulsory drug testing – now!" But those who gather are, for the most part, all mates and pretty soon I change tack and spend the time not speaking, but leaning on my ladder having a chat. Occasionally the handful swells to a crowd of twenty or more, and I go into speaking mode and attempt to recreate the fantasy. After three failures I understand that my motives are flawed and I'm grateful for the company I've got.

There's a minor disturbance when a young black regular runs an alleged racist out of the park directly in front of us. At first the pursued man runs towards the safety of the police but changes his mind when he hears "They won't help you – black man's got his rights now," and he changes his direction and exits. During this a young Mediterranean-looking woman, who's been listening for some time, comes and stands very close to me as if for protection. She smiles and returns to her place when the assumed danger has passed. A little later, meeting over, she introduces herself and then in broken English delivers a delightfully unashamed chat-up line, so obvious that even I can't misconstrue it.

The gist of it is that she's a student of English from Portugal and has heard me speak earlier and thinks I speak with my heart. She says she can't find the English words and wishes there was some other way that she could express to me the way she feels. Jimini returns and overhears most of this and waits within earshot quietly amused. I'm quite flattered. I've also been here before and it involves going for a drink and finding out just what sort of priest, therapist, spiritual consultant, father-figure, care worker, or perhaps mature lover is being sought and then acting accordingly. It's always, at least, mildly interesting, but the last time I actually got laid from such a post-park meeting was with a Puerto Rican go-go dancer in 1978. Tonight I've a got a previous appointment, so even a drink is out of the question. I behave like a perfect gent and introduce her to Jimini and tell her that I might see her here another time.

Thursday 7th September 2000

Esprit d'escalier

Esprit d'escalier, I'm reliably informed, roughly translates from the French as 'spirit of the staircase'. It's that 'What I should have said ...' moment of clarity on the stairs when walking away from an argument, a lover's tiff or a bad gig. As an improvising performer, public speaker and someone incapable of keeping his mouth shut whether on stage or off, I'm more than familiar with such moments. One good thing about my line of endeavour is that there's always a next time.

Whiteleys is a renovated Victorian department store in Queensway, now a modern shopping mall. Whoever did the makeover had the good taste to keep intact the glorious sweeping staircase which is the centrepiece of the building's interior design. In the early eighties, when the place was a forgotten derelict, I broke in with a bunch of punks and squatters doing a venue recce for a possible benefit gig. It was damp and dangerous and too big to defend so we rejected it. Nowadays, I use it as an exotic point to rendezvous – bottom of the staircase in Whiteleys.

I'm stood there waiting for a friend, recalling squats past, when I flash on the confrontation with the mouthy estate agent heckler from last Sunday's meeting, and how I'd failed to expose him and his sordid trade, and how instead I'd lost my rag and could only raise my game to a slanging match and insult him. And worse than that, after he'd stomped off, I made a bollocks of explaining property and the housing market to the rest of the crowd. It's been a tape whirring in my head ever since.

It's been four days and on a staircase only indirectly connected, but the revelation arrives and I realise 'what I should have said was ...'

Sunday 10th September 2000

Mission and motive

I'm no longer pursuing the role of Advocate Heckler. It can remain as a byline on my noticeboard and as a playful aside if anyone insists. Instead, I'm following my creative instincts and concentrating my energy on exploring my own moral dilemmas and deconstructing the local house-style of public speaking.

My artistic mission now, is to combine the ranter and the fool. As a ranter my honesty can often appear earnest, and my confidence is rightly perceived as arrogance. I'm not about to radically change this, merely curb and 'send up' my excesses and present them as parody but without discrediting or diminishing the main bulk of the content. At best my fool has humility and devilment and is expressed in larky asides, qualifications and a range of non-verbal mugging and mimicking. My task is to orchestrate the two essential and conflicting sides of my personality; shift seamlessly from one voice to the other. I will be the first to laugh and make light of my own seriousness and the first to censure the messing about.

Eventually I want to manipulate large crowds of people, get them to believe one thing, then undermine it and get them to believe the opposite, then introduce a lateral third option, until finally they don't know what to believe.

First I must warm up on those whose belief systems depend on low-flying dodgy logic, are embedded in personal emotional trauma, or are perhaps motivated by something more profound that I've yet to discover and may never understand.

Mohammed deflated

St Paul is not around, so I check in my valuables and go and listen to Mohammed the Muslim Sage. This week, for the first time, I'm obliged to heckle him when he refers to whales and dolphins as unintelligent lowly creatures. When I tell him that he's gone down in my estimation, he gives me a dismissive smile 'like he should worry' but I know he can't like hearing such things said honestly. He follows up by retreating to the Koran and quoting from it. I'm disappointed with him. I get quite stroppy and tell him that we have learned many important things about life on this planet since that book was first conceived in the eighth century and it's time for him to wise up. He definitely doesn't like that. I walk away with a bit of a spring in my step, but also a little sad, as you'd expect from a novice one-upping a local guru even if he is ten years younger than me.

'Characters'

Some speakers don't speak that much and are categorised locally as loonies. I prefer to call them 'characters'. Peter is the sole protagonist of the Christian Atheist platform; he often surrounds himself with boards quoting lines from every leading creed and cult. He only speaks when spoken to and although he might appear surreal, his manner is that of a helpful librarian.

Two weeks ago he seemed to be talking a lot of scholarly sense when he told me he could trace the lineage of his belief system back to a branch of Protestantism in the early nineteenth century, although this week he denied this and said it only really surfaced in the 1960s in the USA. Somebody else told me he's a casualty of Roman Catholicism. He's certainly one for the religious trainspotters.

Bob Doom is a friendly soul who wears a tatty sandwich board bearing the legend 'It's going to get worse' around his neck. Despite some evidence to the contrary, I have to agree with him. He says very little

© Ishmahil Blagrove

Christian atheism

unless pressed, but seems to have found his niche keeping people's spirits buoyant by walking around greeting regulars and smiling to everyone else.

Likewise Happy Larry, a gentle, skinny wisp of man in his fifties, who spends much of his Sunday stood on a milk crate dancing, smiling at passers-by and singing old pop songs. I stand and listen to him and ask him questions, knowing that he is something of an anthropologist if you can get him talking. Within five minutes he is entertaining a small crowd of a dozen or so, and describing the courtship rituals and mating habits of the human species – excellent value.

Bob Doom

© Grant Geary

I step up to speak and find myself surrounded by antagonistic hecklers. Sometimes it happens like that. One of them, an over-contributing Latino called Mal who visits maybe once a month and always stands by my side offering unsolicited support, is in particularly rowdy form. He feels obliged to oppose virtually everything I say, and when I pull him about it he tells me "How else da people gonna hear all your brilliant put-me-downs?"

Another irregular who turns up this week is Upperclass Peter, an ageless, six foot six, blonde haired, witty layabout who even as an audience member is a dilettante. Sometimes he is sat astride his neat fold-up bike lazily sniping from the side of the meeting just long enough to have a disruptive impact; then he wanders off only to reappear a little later at the front of the meeting heckling and exercising his birthright to be the centre of attention. For all this, I quite like him. He's mellowed in recent years and, like many rich parasites, he's learned that he can afford to be friendly and affable.

It's one of the biggest and rowdiest meetings I've held this summer. I revel in it, holding several threads together at the same time. Informing the proceedings is an idea around confronting clichés and jargon, which was introduced a couple of weeks ago and now appears to have a life of it's own. People are repeating things with a question mark and heckling each other. The topical issue that demands to be discussed is the planned protests next week by truckers and farmers over the price of petrol. This ends up in a shouting match over whether the ozone layer is depleted more by farting cows than by farting cars which, as a vegetarian cyclist, I chair from the moral high ground. I officially coin my new cliché to describe farming and agriculture – the agri/pesti biz. Meanwhile it stays topical when we're discussing the artist's role in society; some philistine begrudges Social Security benefit to socially excluded artists, so I compare my £47 Housing Benefit to the extra £47 million given to the Millennium Dome this week. I remind the meeting that we agreed to refer to Housing Benefit as Landlord Subsidy. We didn't of course, it's not that sort of meeting, but it's my way of introducing the idea again and giving everybody a sense of continuation. I extemporise: "The power of language, comrades. Housing Benefit accounts for a large chunk of the Social Security budget – billions. If it became common parlance to call it Landlord Subsidy, that alone could change the nature of the housing market. 'Landlord Subsidy', two words – a tiny homeopathic dose subtly administered into the body politic."

Property is theft, property is liberty, property is impossible

Property. I'm back on a subject so familiar that it tripped me up last week, and I have now thought out a fresh approach. There's always a next time, and this is it …

It takes twenty minutes of daft answers and banter, but the gist of it is a question that I ask, in the style of Yusef, to all corners of the big crowd. "What oppresses you the most? Not petrol prices. What gives you the most grief? What do you wake up far too early for? And work far too hard for? Five, six days a week? What steals the largest part of your income each and every week?"

Some suggest the correct answer – rent and mortgage – immediately, but I choose to ignore them and get those with the wrong answer to reconsider. I don't let up until everybody has agreed and it's been settled that 'rent and mortgage' is the answer. Then I ask for actual details and discover that some people are paying over £200 a week – two thirds of their income – and they have no security of tenure. More outrageous is the fact that the poorest pay the largest proportion. Of course they do.

"Property is *the* political issue. You ask me what is property? Property is theft. Property is liberty. Property is impossible. A paradox. What is property? If you are a sentient being treading lightly on this Earth and treating it with respect as a common treasure house for all, then property is impossible. If you pay a peppercorn rent for a secure tenancy that you are happy to call your home, then property is liberty. But if you spend you life working in a job you hate just to earn the money to pay the mortgage or rent the premises that you'd be glad to see the back of, then your life has been stolen from you and property is theft.

"There's more homes out there than they could ever find punters to fill. It's all been built and paid for, most of it several times over. Come on, you know what makes the biggest hole in your income. In all sanity, what's the cost – a bit for maintenance and a bit for a rainy day and the rest is for the landlord to go and play with on the stock-market-correction-money-markets-casino-same-thing? So if you want something to protest about, get your priorities right. Property is theft. Protest about that!"

Virtually everything I say is thought provoking, witty or insightful; and it can go anywhere. I've been doing this particular subject matter for years. Occasionally I give voice to a neat truncated version – a 'first time' which spells out the essentials in a short rant or a burst of set ups and responses; but it's only now that I've prefixed it with such a simple, inclusive and potent question and answer routine.

Unlike Mohammed, I haven't got a Koran to retreat into, or a Christian Bible, or a political party line; but I am stringing together a bunch of provocative arguments with flexible structures that, with luck, I can customise for all occasions.

A little later I manage, at last, to launch into a fairly coherent (and flexible) version of my prophesy on the state of the media and cyber space but this time I concentrate on the optimistic flipside – the quantum leap in the quality of human communication and intimate performance.

By way of bringing it that much closer, I try and introduce a bit of democracy into the proceedings. I'm strong on enthusiasm but a bit short on subtlety. Teaching people how to recognise a woo-cue doesn't catch on, and neither does urging the quieter members of the crowd to secretly hiss when they disagree with hecklers. It finally gets very ragged when people start booing each other and arguing, and the last ten minutes of the two hours is like a football terrace rehearsing for a pantomime. No worries – there's always a next time.

Internecine squabbles
Whenever arch heckler The Appalling Lurch, master of the snide put-down, heckles sexually obsessive speaker Martin Besserman, it quickly ends in the latter having a tantrum, stepping down from his ladder, and refusing to speak. But it doesn't stop there. Martin then wanders round whinging and soliciting for political allies wherever he can find them, hoping to somehow censure Lurch and have an unofficial restraining order put on him. Lurch follows up saying very little, displaying a shrug of contempt and a self-righteous grin on his fat face. This mutual hatred has a long history, and neither of them comes out of it very well. More pertinently, it's got nothing to do with me and I can't think why I bother to get involved, but I do. I make a point of talking to them both separately. I tell Martin that I personally find his adolescent boasting about sexual conquests irritating and for the sexually deprived it must be a red rag to a bull. I tell Lurch that I find his venomous tongue the ugliest thing about him, and also I reckon he's clearly jealous of Martin's prowess as a speaker and maybe even as a stud. When he starts to argue and tell me that he's happily married, I realise how small-time-piddley the whole thing is and that he and Martin probably deserve each other. Worse still, I come out of it like some meddling busybody.

Situation vacant – great white hope

I am beginning to recognise a small constituency at the Corner who are not served by the current crop of speakers. They are like a meeting in waiting. They mooch about, have a bit of a moan to each other and heckle to pass the time. What they are waiting for is that which in sport is always characterised as the 'great white hope'. It's here too, lurking in the fantasies of many a sad old git – the generation before mine, who were too young to fight in the Second World War but too old to be teenagers and part of the rock n roll generation. They have nothing, they've always had nothing, but they are white and thoroughly male, and that alone once meant something. They can remember a time when homosexuals were illegal and when blacks, Asians, Irish and foreigners in general either didn't exist or knew their place, alongside women and teenagers, as second class citizens.

Arguments for equal opportunities and multiculturalism are forcing them to share their nothing with everybody else. Every Sunday afternoon, they crawl out of the woodwork and turn up at Speakers' Corner constituting little fading pockets of nostalgia that know the past will not

© Ishmahil Blagrove

return. They resemble forlorn auditions for Waiting for Godot. They don't ask for much, they no longer crave an Oswald Mosley, their demands are not for immigrants to be repatriated or perverts to be flogged, they certainly can't be doing with the donning of brown shirts, fisticuffs or fascist salutes, but if someone vaguely white could just come down here for an hour or so, stand in front of them and not slag them off, and maybe read a few Daily Mail headlines out aloud, it would brighten up their Sunday afternoons. Bless.

Sunday 17th September 2000

Shortly after my arrival, I meet Andre from the London Arts Board, while I'm still passing the time of day with St Paul. We then meet Claire, who is my LAB advisor. They were obviously coming down for a quiet peek, and bumping into me on arrival wasn't part of their plot. They're a little embarrassed and don't want to cramp my style any further, so I suggest they go and check out Martin, Ishmahil and Heiko. No sooner have they left than Francis, from the publishers Gothic Image, arrives. She's buying me dinner later, and we're going to talk over a little book deal. All this should be added pressure, but it's not. I can feel myself rising to the occasion.

I've been doing a lot of thinking in the past week, mulling over the ethics of manipulating the crowd and how much of my agenda to reveal. I've decided to treat the meeting like I'd treat a child asking about sex. I'll answer questions honestly, but not give more information than is actually required. When in doubt tell the truth.

Positive warm-up
I wander out among the meetings socialising and heckling. Whether or not I am unconsciously trying to earn good favour with the muse, I'm not sure, but I find myself making only positive interventions. Mohammed the Muslim Sage sighs when he sees me and greets me warily. I confound his expectations and heckle his hecklers.

Guru Barry is being heckled mercilessly by a good-natured crowd, and when I arrive he jokingly throws his arms up in despair. "Oh no. I can't deal with you as well," he pleads. So I pitch in and support him too.

Ali is reading out a deliberately confusing tract to thirty bewildered listeners. I can't make head nor tail of it either, but I berate those who leave his meeting.

"No staying power. Slackers! You have to put the time in, if you want to reap the profound rewards of the message. I've got to go now Ali."

Guru Barry catharting

I set up opposite Ali, and far enough along the railings from where the old Sufi Mystic is dozing in his deck chair so as not to disturb him and have him jump up behind me and cause disruption. I embrace my feeling of ridiculous confidence and bark a crowd: "Friends, lovers, comrades and fellow creatures. The revolution starts here."

A small crowd gathers in front of me. I confide in them with a smile "I'm hot! I'm dangerous! You've been warned."

I take off with much the same flair as I did last week but this week, with the stakes seemingly higher, I soar. I have long sequences of orchestrating the contributions from the floor – repeating questions and answering them, recapping arguments and moving them on, sometimes juggling several themes at the same time.

"What am I doing here? Why do I habitually drag myself down here every Sunday? Eh? Eh? Why did you come here today? Why? Why do we choose to hang out here? Nothing on the telly? No. Wrong. There's the same old shit on the telly. It's no worse on Sundays. But thank you for your contribution. Plug your brain in before you open you mouth next time. No! No offence. Just establishing some guidelines for the standard of heckling. Why would I be doing that? Why are we here? Eh? Anybody? For the women? No, I don't believe you. Unless you fell out of bed this morning, looked in the mirror and said 'I know. I won't wash. I won't bother to shave, I'll put me old work jeans on with that baggy blue T-shirt, the one with the stain I've been wearing all week and I'll go down the Park, stand next to Tony, and some of his charisma might rub off on me and I'll pull women.' Probably not. So why are you here? Alright, a clue. Not 'sexual intercourse' but? Anybody? 'Sex in the afternoon'. No. 'Sexual harassment'. No. Hang on! Hang on! One moron at a time. Fair enough. Sorry. One sentient being at a time. Right. You, the moron in the bobble hat. No. No. Forget all about women. No, this is not the homosexual meeting. Alright. I'll tell you. Not 'sexual intercourse' but 'social intercourse'. That's why we're here – communication. For one reason or another, you came down here today to communicate with each other. So, how was it for you?"

Mixed Ability Shaman

What makes today's performance a landmark for me is the complexity of my 'attitude'. I manage to successfully integrate several voices: the serious orator, didactic and long-suffering; the loose cannon ranter, unhinged and messianic; the fool, larky, lateral and self-deprecating, and the down-to-earth geezer quipping asides in a running commentary to his mates.

"This is Speakers' Corner. The so-called bastion of free speech. This place is unique. What we have here is a culture of licence and familiarity where you can approach complete strangers and engage in conversations which can just as easily develop into profound communion as a heated slanging match. True. Check it out missus, ms, sir. Beg pardon.

"It's taken hundreds of years to evolve. So don't abuse it – participate! Make a contribution. Any questions? No, not you! You've said too much already. No. He has. He's getting on my tits and I've only been up here ten minutes. This man here is an over-contributor. He's got over the first hurdle. He knows how to express himself. It's the next bit he's got major problems with – the content. What has he got to express? Jack Shit squared! "Before we can have free speech, we have to have individuals capable of expressing themselves and they've got to have something to say. So, apart from you, any questions? Shut it! Give the tourists a chance. Alright people, I tell you what I'll do. I'll give you all a brief go. One word. Then you can go back home to wherever it is, and say I went to Speakers' Corner in London and I didn't stand there like a lemon, I participated! Dine out for months on it, they will. Now, If you disagree with anything I've said then you can shout out 'bollocks'. No, not bollocks, that'll involve the police and they are quite capable of involving themselves. Shout out 'rubbish'. On the other hand, if you agree with what I'm saying, shout out something affirmative. Yes, very funny, 'something affirmative'. Just imagine the brain behind that comment. Eh? Oi! If you carry on getting bigger laughs than me, you'll get a slap. That was a woo-cue. But first things first. Your chance for a spot of self-expression – 'Rubbish' or 'Yeah'. Wait for it. Wait for it. Wait for it.

"Friends, Lovers, Comrades, Fellow creatures. What do think of it so far?

"Let me hear you say 'Yeah!'

"Let me hear you say 'Yeah! Yeah!'

"Let me hear you say 'Bahhhh!'"

The large crowd once again brings more than its fair share of speakers and regulars – snipers – waiting their chance to impress the crowd with a well-timed heckle. At times I am dealing with a chorus of hecklers, some serious, some silly and some devious. I'm enjoying it, and I don't hide the fact.

Ishmahil and an accomplished sniper, Maxwell, take up positions in the front of the meeting. It's a long time since Ishmahil has done this and I reckon it's indicative of my growing status as a speaker. He heckles me with a joke that I heard on the television last night. What's the difference between petrol and paraffin? The answer is 'There is no f in petrol'. But I turn it round on him. Last week, I had suggested that he repeat questions, so the crowd get to hear the set up and his punchline or comment. I reply in a way that sounds as if I am going to do much the same, but let him add the punch.

"What is the difference between … the joke I heard that stupid camp television presenter tell last night? … And the one you were about to crack? The answer: 'There is no fucking difference'."

It gets a big laugh, especially from Maxwell who high-fives Ishmahil urging him to laugh as well. I see all this, of course, and I rub it in. Getting very cocky with it, I add: "Oh yes. You're playing with the big boys now."

Ishmahil leaves soon after, but he'll be back. Max stays for some time enjoying himself and in a welcome supportive role.

Albert makes his first contribution – a silly heckle. I tell him that he must attempt to be sensible and that he can try again later. He mumbles something else that I don't hear but assume is silly, leaving me no alternative but to give him a public warning. I explain: "He's already been warned on numerous previous occasions. Albert. One more silly heckle and you'll get a slap. It's for his own good. No, we've tried giving him a hug and it just makes him worse."

The Brotherhood of the Cross and Star

Later on Albert says something sensible and I take the credit for his improvement. I also take the opportunity to tell any parents listening that threats of mild violence only work with subjects "Who should know better. Albert! If he really was stupid, how come he knows when I insult his intelligence? If you can't love them, you can at least try to be honest."

Cynical James graces my meeting for the first time. He comes out with a crap pun, and I repeat the mantra.

"If you can't love them. At least be honest. Now you are an intelligent man, but you choose to be shallow and disruptive. Why is this? I reckon

© Zac Zacharides

it's because you're a frustrated speaker. I reckon you should go and have a word with yourself."

He accuses me of being too serious. I check myself. I am being serious. The Nigerian preacher in the white smock has just started his meeting and is screeching incoherently close by. I tell James that I'm an antidote to all the other meetings, which are very silly and get a laugh by indicating my new neighbour.

An Asian heckler showing off in front of his family does a coarse piss-take of my accent. As it happens I've recently been giving a lot of thought to racism and this sort of slack and have coincidentally been up all night writing a piece on the subject. It's very fresh with me. I adopt a version of cockney at the edge of my authentic range. I'm reading my reply off the virtual page in my head.

"That's a very cheap approximation of my complex speech patterns and highly idiosyncratic London accent. Now I understand that you are, in some way, indulging in a primitive payback ritual in retaliation for the very real racism you've experienced (and many continue to experience) in your own life. Now, do you think I'm going to allow my white guilt to double bind me into making a paternal concession, where you get to do funny cockney piss-takes unchallenged?"

I slip into exaggerated Peter Sellars' Indian doctor. "That would be highly unlikely, my old chapati. Highly unlikely."

He laughs and so does everybody else laugh. My ego meanwhile is wishing I'd caught Maxwell or Ishmahil with a variation of this routine. But there's always a next time.

Petrol protests

Last week, a heckler in a wheelchair took exception to my views on the work ethic, and this week he's back with an observation about the fuel crisis. His question may sound tongue in cheek, but I know that he actually disapproves of me profoundly.

"See what happens when you tell the people to stop working. See the sort of anarchy you get."

We are back on the petrol protests again and suddenly everyone's got an opinion. I quickly get it on to my agenda.

"So, what have we learned? We've learned that all that's needed for a modest revolution is a bunch of oiks in big motors blocking the driveways to a few petrol stations and the whole country is brought to its knees and the government panics and starts thinking about conceding to its demands. It's a piece of piss, a doddle, and what we've learned is that if that's all it takes, then we'd better start increasing our demands. Why bother with a few pence off the price of petrol when we can have anything. What oppresses you the most? What do you really want changed?"

I'm soon on familiar material and urging more protests at the petrol stations, but this time demanding the abolition of rents and mortgages and ...

"England! England! If this is my country, then I want my three and half acres Now! Alright I know it's only two acres when you do all the sums. But basic trade union negotiating strategy – always demand more than you're willing to accept."

Saudi oil and the electric car

The subject of the protests continues with spin-offs ranging from the fragility of the short-supply globalised economy and the money markets, to charging up a twelve-volt car battery with an exercise bike. The session culminates in an inspired sequence memorable for the sophistication of the participation.

"How many people here have got an electric car? How many people have seen an electric car? Milk floats. Yes. Fifty years ago milk floats were poodling along at twelve miles per hour. And they still are. Yes. Why is that? Why hasn't that technology been developed? No, it's not because it's crap. It works. The patent. Ah! And who's got the patent? Who owns the patent on the electric car? Alright, you tell me. Who's got the most petrol? 'Oil' yeah. Petrol, oil, same thing. No, not 'the petrol stations'. They only have enough for a couple of days, then the tanker has to come round and fill 'em up again. 'The oil companies'. Warmer but 'No'. 'The Arabs'. Warmer, but not all Arabs. Sarti over there. He's an Arab, but he hasn't got any petrol or oil, apart from a couple of pints in the tank of his moped.

"'Saddam Hussein', 'Iraq', 'Texas', 'Kuwait'. Still only warm. Think about it. 'Saudi Arabia'. Good. Thank you Eric. Eric here – man with handlebar 'tache – he is your role model. He's thinking. But he's not thinking hard enough, are you Eric? It's not the country of Saudi Arabia that owns the oil is it? It's the ...? 'The Saudi Royal Family'. Correct. Is it the Saudi Royal Family that's got the deeds to the ranch? Yes, okay. Yes I know 'Texas has got loads of oil' but they're Americans and they're all too fat and lazy or virtual and delicate to get their hands dirty pumping it out.

"Right what was the original question? No, before that. We've been there. We've done that. You've told me who owns most of the oil. Now, the original question was ... ? No. Nothing to do with 'sexual intercourse'. It's time for your cold shower. Thank you. Yes. Patent on the electric car. Well done. Sticky star for you. Who owns the patent on the electric car? And the answer is? Repeat that please, 'The Saudi Royal Family'. Now I didn't say that. You said that. Let me understand again what this meeting is saying.

The Saudi Royal Family owns the patent on the electric car. No. I never said it. Eric said it. Course it's not the truth. It's just something concocted in this meeting. Is it true? I don't know. You tell me. You made it up.

"It is true as it happens."

"No it's not."

This manipulation is getting lots of laughter, and the quality of the attention is something I've not experienced before. The mood is expressed by a delighted statement from the floor.

"You're playing with our minds."

That's when I start to get cocky "What? Don't be silly. A speaker playing with your minds? That sort of thing doesn't happen here. This is Speakers' Corner. It's in a rut. We're all Jesus freaks and nutters down here."

"So? What's the truth?" asks a frustrated heckler.

"The truth, my friend, is a beautiful thang."

"Does the Saudi Royal Family own the patent on the electric car?" he repeats.

"I don't know" I say. "That's your homework."

I now decide to stop. This is another advance because I stop when I'm winning, rather than when it fizzles out. Maybe I should only ever do short sessions of an hour or ninety minutes, and then stop.

Heckling technique

I'm still full of myself though and wanting to show off a bit more when I notice Paddy the Christian and his little crew supporting one of their new recruits on a high ladder, making what looks like a maiden speech. Paddy is a big cheerful avuncular man with a smile for everyone, but some of his minions are often the opposite – very uptight. I don't know where he finds them, but I wouldn't want to hang out there. This fledgling preacher looks like he could be a bouncer at the Mean Fiddler. He's a serious sinner in a smart leather jacket, booming out hellfire and damnation to no audience. I try out my version of Irish Chris's heckling style, and it works. A crowd is gathering. I stand beneath him, repeating bits of his text in mock innocence, strongly disapproving of the imagery.

"'Burn in hell?' He can't say that can he? That's terrible, that! That's an horrendous image. That'll upset people. 'Eternal torment?' Oh No! Paddy. Don't let him say any more. There's women and children present."

Paddy and co are not happy with my intervention and get really annoyed when I start apologising on behalf of the speaker and explaining to the crowd.

"He doesn't mean it people. You're not going to actually burn forever. It's only symbolic. Tell 'em Paddy."

After ten minutes, I've pulled a crowd of about thirty and for the second time I decide to stop while I'm ahead.

I've definitely made my mark this week. My only critique of my own performance is that I am still hard-edged and defensive. I must mellow and soften and continue learning how to play.

Sunday 24th September 2000

It's been a day of hit and run thunderstorms and I'm attending Speakers' Corner without my bike, ladder or noticeboard. Later on I'm travelling by public transport to Hoxton Hall where some friends are involved in an experimental Commedia dell'arte troupe.

Martin revisited

I arrive on foot in bright sunshine immediately after a downpour. There's a few hundred hardy souls spread around a few speakers. Martin Besserman has the largest meeting of about forty people. Recently word has got back to Martin about the way I have been describing him in my off-the-cuff reviews of other speakers. Word has got back to me that Martin believes I've judged him unfairly. I decide to take this opportunity to reappraise him. I approach from behind and observe unnoticed for as long as possible. It's about ten or fifteen minutes before he discovers my presence, and what I witness in the interim only underlines my worst expectations.

The subject matter concerns chatting-up foreign women. He asks a woman tourist where she comes from and she replies "Sydney, Australia." Then he explains the subtext of this exchange to the overwhelmingly male crowd. "When you ask a woman where they are from and they tell you, it means they want to shag you."

The crowd laugh. The Australian woman, momentarily shocked, also laughs. But her laughter is nervous and forced. She is trying to laugh it off. Martin's only concession to put right any awkwardness she might be feeling is to now attack the men in the audience for being inadequate. "She wouldn't have told you, you or you. Would you?"

She's the only woman in a meeting of men and she has decided to brazen it out.

"You wouldn't shag him would you?" he asks her.

"I don't want to shag anyone" she declares, unwittingly opening up the next subject, which is inevitably 'lesbians'. She stands her ground and laughs off yet more banter, including some prurient dildo jokes. Martin is at his worst when he is playing to the rabble like this. I find it all really objectionable, but for Martin, and his regular crowd, it's just marking time with familiar material until the maestro pulls something out of the bag. And he does.

What happens next is much of the same contentwise, but technically it's a stroke of brilliance. From his vantage point he notices two young women approaching; they are unseen by the crowd, who he now primes with a few familiar lines about his own sexual potency, leaving an expectation that he will prove his claims. The cohorts may recognise the routine but they can't guess the denouement. Then, just as the two women pass close by, he speaks to them over the top of the meeting in a friendly and disarming manner. "Hello, Hello," he beams to each of them.

"Hello" says one of them

"And where are you from?"

"Turkey!" She replies innocently, instigating a big laugh.

"See! All women want to shag me." He says looking round the meeting triumphantly. He catches my eye and acknowledges me with a winning smile.

I'm at my most priggish. I shake my head disapprovingly and leave.

He thinks I'm a condescending old git and I think he's an adolescent about to have a mid-life crisis. There's probably no hope for either of us.

No progress there then.

People have been arriving all the time. Ishmahil has a large lively crowd and Guru Barry, Mohammed the Muslim Sage and the Nigerian Christian in the white robe, share the remainder. While I watch, several other speakers start up.

I've never noticed it before, but the laughter associated with schadenfreude has a quality all of it's own. A frothy drunkenness pervades Ishmahil's meeting. Half the gathering appear to be helpless with laughter. It's only when I acclimatise that I understand the source of the amusement. A drunk and dishevelled Irish Christian, with a gaping potbelly is sentimentally slurring biblical quotes as if he were singing Country and Western. He wants to mount the ladder – not a good idea. Ishmahil gently deters him and turns him round to face the crowd and he slowly slumps to the ground. Ishmahil does little more than shake his head and corpse sympathetically to elicit more laughter.

Bob 'it's going to get worse' Doom is very perky and assures me that, throughout the rages of the storm, a presence was maintained. He tells me this as a matter of pride, comrade to comrade, as if some unbroken chain of events linked to the past has been heroically kept intact. Socialist Nick, a solid and reliable eyewitness, is nodding affirmatively. So there's no doubt about it.

"Are you going to speak?" says Nick. I am suddenly back in wobbly land and fighting off an attack of performance anxiety – the speaker's fear of mass rejection. I'm looking round for reasons to be excused from duty. The sun is bright, the crowds are gathering and there's even an available bread rack (wider but lower than a milk crate). There's no way out. "Yeah

Ishmahil

man. I'm there," I say without conviction. We stand in silence for a short while and then, as a useless delaying tactic, I go through a bizarre little ritual of offering the plinth to each of them in turn. Nick shuns it as if it's something out of his range. Bob has given it more thought, "No, no. I could never do it. I haven't got the confidence." I actually egg him on and tease him with it. Finally, I pull myself together and stop projecting my own fear. We all have our part to play. I couldn't do what Bob does – stand around all day wearing a homemade sandwich board. I stake my claim to the bread rack, kick it and follow it across the tarmac for twenty yards drawing attention to myself.

I start off tentatively with the 'freespeech/individuals with something to say' rant developed last week, and pull a crowd of twenty including Grant, who has just recently launched a web page for the rough sleepers – hungryandhomeless.com, featuring a full colour picture of William and his album covers.

Life and death

When I ask for 'any questions', it's Grant who responds with a thoughtful "Should the law override the wishes of parents?" The media have been full of this all week. A couple from Malta have come to the UK for the birth of their conjoined twins, one half of which is unlikely to survive more than a few months, precipitating the death of the other. The doctors want to intervene immediately, kill the weaker twin to save the stronger. The parents are against the doctors cutting their child in two but the law backs the doctors. I immediately relax; I've been pondering this one all week and have been wondering if I might get a chance to talk it out at the Park. I explain the question and moral dilemma, assume a chairing role and open it out for discussion. It's after listening to the rag-bag of contributions and, more pertinently, who is making them that I find myself profoundly sympathising with the unfashionable position of defending the parents wishes. It's not long before I'm putting a convincing argument together. Twenty people are listening intently, including a hard core half-dozen vociferously pitched against me.

As far as I'm concerned, Jeffrey discredits his 'kill one to save the other' position by his statement that there should have been an abortion as soon as the situation was known. Follow that logic.

A youngster likens the situation to a motorcycle and sidecar. I tell him to find a more appropriate metaphor, only to launch into a pretty far-fetched one of my own.

"Should American culture be cut away from the global body politic to allow the rest of humanity to live a reasonable life?"

An ironic American responds with "So you agree that America actually has some culture?"

Nick is obsessed with making it into a religious issue, seeing the parents as dim-witted puppets of the Catholic Church. This leads me to outline a hypothetical scenario with intelligent, sensitive parents.

A couple are traumatised by the nature of their progeny. They love and recognise the two fragile beings struggling to live in one abnormal body. They understand that the life exists only because of medical science. They want to spend the few months of the twin's short life discovering a loving communion. This can help them come to terms with the inevitable grief. Also, the complexity of the experience and effect on their relationship demands that they be there for each other with no other agendas.

Then, the government tells them that they have no rights in the situation and that the surgeons are coming in to kill one child and save the other. There is no certainty as to how that might pan out. Imposing on the parents a profoundly disturbing alternative to the one they are set on is criminal. They ought to be left alone; they have enough traumas. For me, it comes down to the clarity of the quality of life. I also sense there is less of a taboo about killing than there is about death and dying.

The second half of the meeting takes a different turn and gets quite playful at times. I particularly liked hearing a young Kosovan student correct Albert's English grammar. Another thing that has become established is that I don't smoke tobacco when Eric with the handlebar 'tache is present. It came out of me saying that I welcomed reasons to stop smoking.

Towards the end of the meeting, six police walk past in Indian file. Nick shouts something and hums the Laurel and Hardy theme tune. I know I'm getting tired when I can't be bothered to join in. I close the meeting after it has dwindled to a handful.

Bad timing – bold intentions.

A trendy-looking Asian woman introduces herself – Chatti. Do I remember her? I don't! Turns out she was a shaven-headed punk in one of my workshops eight years ago. Now she's a very attractive thirty something. I may not remember her, but she certainly remembers my workshop, especially the monitoring scheme. She's monitored my performance today. I question her eagerly. This is both a review of my workshop techniques and my speaking performance.

"Dynamics?"

"Paid too much attention to the hecklers up the front at the expense of those trying to follow the plot up the back."

"Attitude?"

"A sensitive, politically correct, bully."

"Material?"

"Heavy-duty, thought-provoking."

This woman has been paying attention. She's also bright and attractive and she has approached me. I've not followed through twice this summer, and here I am again about to say 'Good to meet you, take care, have a nice life.' So I don't. I try it on – Contemporary Commedia Dell'arte in Hoxton should be just up her alley.

"Diction?"

"Good."

"Timing?"

"Good?"

"Fancy a drink?"

"Not now, I'm with my husband."

"Fair enough." I laugh, a little embarrassed and apologetic.

"I said 'not now', I didn't say 'no'."

Sunday 1st October 2000

Sleepwalking in Baker Street on a British Sunday

Almost thirty years of avoiding regular work and pursuing a nocturnal life style of variously a writer, nightclub comedian, and sometimes an unashamed layabout has taken its toll on my system; my sleep patterns are irredeemably stuck – I don't do mornings. As a loose rule I sleep from 5am until about one in the afternoon.

Baker Street, 9.30am local time. I step off an Easy Jet coach from Luton Airport en route home from Amsterdam. I'm experiencing the familiar mild euphoria that comes with having not slept – I'm knackered. The sun is very bright, and the streets appear strangely clean and vacant. I walk slowly, lugging my bags due south, knowing I'll eventually hit Oxford Street. I've never seen Speakers' Corner at this time of day and if I can stay awake, I know I'm going to enjoy it.

Speakers' Corner is home ground for me. I know at least fifty people by name and there's another fifty I probably nod to when I pass them in the street. I've argued, agreed and joked with them; wrong-footed and rabble-roused them; I have a shared culture of gossip, rumour and information, of support and intervention, of borrowed milk crates, exchanged pamphlets, bummed fags, passed joints, slugs of brandy, cups of tea, bottles of water, and a myriad of small favours and old scores. I have many friends and comrades among them and, hopefully less than my fair share of enemies too. There are probably a couple of hundred faces, many of them well-defined personalities who, as far as I'm concerned, are Speakers' Corner. So it's shocking to the point of being eerie and unreal to arrive shortly after 10am and find the place heaving with activity but to not recognise a soul; and not be recognised by a soul either. Such a dreamlike experience certainly wakes me up. There are totally different speakers with totally different hecklers and even totally different local loonies. Nothing is familiar except some of the banter. Mildly elated, I wander about like the lead character in a sci-fi story looking for a familiar face in a parallel universe, but there is none. I do actually pinch myself

Time-zone tourist

There is so much to take in. There's a formality about the meetings, and I'm acutely aware of people's politeness. Clearly, the earlier shift attracts a much nicer class of person. Like the vacant streets around Baker Street, it feels vaguely old fashioned. The spirit of the British Sunday is alive and well and, as befits the institution, you have to get out of bed early in the morning to experience it. I feel like I'm an extra on a Disney film set of Speakers' Corner. There's no rabid chanting, although a gathered church with a corduroy preacher is holding a little service with constant prayers. Someone is singing somewhere, but they don't sound drunk. In fact nobody's drunk, or stoned. There's no bunch of backpackers sprawled on the grass, no lads barging around egging each other on. There is still plenty of promenading but it ain't so sexy, and the police are at a distance, directing tourists and suchlike: they

© Ishmahil Blagrove

are not suspiciously nosing around the bigger meetings in small groups. Apart from the local rough sleepers there's a distinct lack of the disreputable.

Several young men, all born-again Christians, are publicly confessing their sins and urging their small congregations to do the same. I venture my first heckle to a fresh-faced innocent with hardly any audience.

"You know when you do something with a friend, and it doesn't feel like 'sin', it actually feels quite nice, especially if you both practice and get really accomplished, and then the pleasure you give each other increases each time you do it and you become willing slaves to each other's desires and learn how to sustain the ecstasy and it gets wilder and wilder and then every time you do it you always start screaming, and crying tears of pure joy … and you have such exquisite memories, yeah? Is that still a sin then?"

To his credit, he treats it like the joke it is and laughs.

World government

I move on and listen to a tweedy old gent with wavy grey hair and woolly liberal opinions, who is advocating Democratic World Government to a large crowd. He's in the Lord Soper mould – decent and paternal and it's only after I hear him deal with a few questions that I feel confident enough to heckle.

"With respect squire, democracy has to start at the other end of the dung heap. Until people have control over their own living situations, their own work arrangements and their own lives, it doesn't matter a toss if you vote in another layer of suits to smile for the cameras."

I get a little round of applause for this contribution. The old boy has hardly started his reply, which is very wordy, when he is heckled with "Never mind all that old codswallop! How's your wife and my three kids?"

The speaker is too 'British Sunday' to give the reply, 'They've still all got syphilis' but instead apologises to the crowd for the coarseness of the heckler and then tries to patronise him into silence.

Born Again Christian Cowboys

A little later the same heckler bursts in on another meeting with the same opening line, this time he gets a good natured slanging match and comes off worse in front of an enormous crowd. I'd heard a lot about the Texas half of the Christian Cowboys and how he was the closest thing to a stand-up comedian at the Park. Well it's true, he stood posing for photographs, cracking very old jokes and bantering with hecklers with the same dedication to entertainment as Martin. With boots, Stetson and a high kitsch white suit with a broad black 'Jesus loves you' pinstripe. His running mate, who I'd seen a few weeks ago, is stood at the side, throwing in heckler put-downs, and helping out occasionally with the photo opportunities. This is an amateur entertainment aimed directly at the tourists. These guys are not deranged or deluded, they are obsessive hobbyists and, despite all the references to Jesus, what they are doing has very little to do with Christianity. The detractors are wrong; Speakers' Corner is not being taken over by religion, it's being invaded by showbiz.

The raucous peripatetic heckler is called Peter. He is on first-name terms with all the regulars and he attacks every speaker as soon as they show themselves. Sometimes, he won't let go and manages to disrupt the meetings, but mostly he seems content to display how loud and obnoxious he can be and then move on. Probably a cry for help.

I hadn't seen Charlene from the lesbian and gay platform for many years and I'd assumed she no longer attended, but suddenly here she is, a little older, occupying a slightly different time zone; still warm and friendly and surrounded as ever by a coterie of young gay men.

Finally I start to recognise more contemporary faces and the parallel universe very gradually starts to mesh with the one I inhabit.

Nicolas the Globe and Red Danny are the first to arrive and break the spell and I watch both of them speak, noting they're on better form than I've ever seen them. Later on they tell me that speaking in the morning is far more civilised and that the later it gets, the madder it gets. Tell me about it.

The Nation of Islam

At twelve noon I am reminded of one of the reasons why I made the effort to come here and not go home to bed. The Nation of Islam sect advocates the separate development ideas of the black American Louis Farrakhan.

Nation of Islam

I've heard so many ominous things about them and their leader, Leo Chester, that I'm quite looking forward to seeing them in the flesh. Chester was, up until quite recently, a stand-up comedian. He confined himself to the Black comedy circuit where he was a regular headliner. His short career peaked with sell out gigs at the Hackney Empire and appearances on the black television comedy show The Real McCoy. So on one level, I've got a lot in common with him; we're both stand-ups turned Hyde Park speakers. This is going to be interesting.

I'm getting very tired and sit on my suitcase, joining the many others who are intent on watching the show right from the beginning. Chester undoubtedly has some charisma, enough to mobilise a posse of eight young male followers all wearing an approximation of a uniform – formal black suits and red bow ties. This is like no other meeting at Speakers' Corner. They erect a makeshift stage from six milk crates and a piece of six foot by four foot plywood, a sentry takes up a position on each corner, the remainder of the team stand in front at ground level looking serious. Chester assumes his position above them, centre stage, standing like a preacher behind a stained wooden lectern. A large crowd is gathering, over half of whom are white and many are first-timers and tourists. Chester, a youngish West Indian probably no older than 35, immediately lays down some ground rules – he will speak first and then there will be time for questions later. This statement, plus the general air of intimidation coming off the surly-looking 'minders', is enough to censure any hecklers. Listening in silence goes against the local grain and when he starts speaking in the confrontational house style (which has developed in concert with heckling) it becomes that much more frustrating. Chester is far from politically gauche. The clarity of his message, the style of delivery, in fact the whole tableau, is calculated to provoke the latent racism in the crowd. Then, to censure any such expression or debate and force it to smoulder in silence, is a further 'let's see how you like it' sophistication in turning the tables on whitey.

His opening fifteen minutes is intended as much for his immediate and potential followers as it is for the rest of us. I don't really understand his explanation that dressing formally gives a black man dignity. Surely wearing what is clearly a uniform is what a lot of black people have always been obliged to do in the narrow range of jobs made available to them. A lot of people, particularly blacks for various reasons, have a strong aversion to uniforms. Or have I missed a salient point? The explanations continue on the subject of vigilante action against racist violence. Chester's argument that the group members need to be ready and able to defend themselves causes a perceptible raising of chins and tightening of chests from those being described. There is a corresponding frisson of concern from a section of the crowd. I automatically check for the presence of the police, as do many others; three officers – all of them white – are observing from a distance, nothing at all threatening – we're still in British Sunday time.

Listening to Chester speak about white people reminds me of listening to radical feminist separatists talk about men, or class warriors talk about the rich, posh and powerful. Or me talk about people who work for a living.

Many black speakers are confusing and apparently confused about who, for the sake of a generalised political argument, actually qualifies as black. I have variously heard Turks, Irish, women and children included as a concession to a persistent heckler. Hardline class warriors were often accused of being 'Proleir than thou'– claiming status from the purity of their working class credentials. A similar syndrome is evident here. Chester is clear: out of Africa blacks are the real McCoy, and of course there is no debate until perhaps at the end of the meeting.

I have a silent word with myself – I am neither going to heckle nor ask a question, for the simple reason that I think I can see what's going on here and the odds are stacked. Chester and his crew are not about to give me any space to establish myself and will quickly characterise me as they please. Also I am nodding off and far from alert.

Right on cue, the raucous heckler arrives and bellows out: "If you don't like it in this country, why don't you clear off back to where you came from." But he doesn't stick around for an answer; this is his parting shot on leaving the Park. Chester chooses not to reply. Instead he pauses briefly, letting it hang in the air, and then continues speaking. The police don't follow through either, like everyone else, they're glad to see the back of an offensive oik. But there it is, if evidence were needed, The Nation of Islam does not exist in a vacuum.

Soon after this a couple of the crew start to participate, supporting the speaker, low-church style, repeating key phrases and by adding their own riffs. "Teach, black man, teach" or they simply start to underline key passages with, "The truth! The truth!" This chorus appears to have a momentum of it's own, although Chester knows how to conduct it. Simply by the emphasis and inflection he chooses for his delivery, he can manipulate the chorus and turn his full stops into a series of big finishes. I'm envious.

The subject matter is, on one level, refreshingly topical with an analysis of this week's media treatment of black issues and updates on the debate about institutionalised racism in the police force and the continuing developments around the Stephen Lawrence inquiry. It's only when he starts explaining and justifying the group's own actions in current campaigns that I begin to see the flaws in the performance and understand the concern of his many detractors. There's more than a hint of paranoia informing his take on events, and he has an overly ambiguous interest in media attention. "The press will be here taking notes. Oh yes, they come here and watch me" he assures us.

"In your dreams" I heckle, quietly and ineffectually, and then quickly remind myself to 'shut it'.

Chester is bright, but he ain't that bright. He makes mistakes, the most important being that no one appears to be pulling him about his mistakes, particularly his immediate crew who appear ready to defend him right or wrong. That makes for a slow learning process and an arrogance that can lead to demagoguery. As a speaker he is not without charm, but he is also strident and earnest to the point of being deliberately humourless. When he does raise a laugh it's carefully directed to his black constituency. This degree of care and contrivance over the delivery of his text requires that he eliminate an important element from his performer's armoury. Without self-deprecation, (universally appreciated by all sections of a crowd) he is denying himself a vital tool which can help lighten his touch, broaden his appeal and give depth and dimension to his attitude. It's a political decision and it's a mistake. On the rare occasions his comedian's intuition does show itself and a spontaneous aside does reveal him as momentarily vulnerable or uncertain, he is quick to re-establish the sombre mood and remind himself, and us, that this is a serious meeting with a serious agenda and there is no cause for laughter. 'The truth' indeed.

It's always a little embarrassing to behold your own frailty exposed in another, especially when it is unchecked and seen as a strength and acknowledged without humility or humour. For a few weeks now, I have been speaking to crowds of between fifty and a hundred and my ego has run riot, my only course has been to explore ways of admitting it publicly, subvert the power trip, mock, enjoy and deconstruct it. That for me, an anarchist with a healthy contempt for leadership and ruling cliques, is a serious mission. Leo Chester's serious mission is set on achieving the opposite goal and he's been pursuing it by speaking regularly for at least eighteen months, and not to larky baying mobs but to censured, receptive and seemingly uncritical audiences of two hundred plus.

There are moments towards the climax of the meeting when he is rabble-rousing his immediate flock and getting carried away by the sound of his own voice, when he coyly lets slip these fantasies of leadership and reveals himself as transparently intent on power. Did I really hear him refer to himself as Leo X?

Chester's ambitions clearly stretch beyond worrying tourists and educating a small congregation on a Sunday morning in the Park. Unlike most speakers, he actively and urgently seeks a full-time political career elsewhere. It's hard to imagine him in a year's time still displaying the same confidence and putting on the same show without having seriously questioned what he's doing and who he's doing it for; especially against the backdrop of Speakers' Corner with its has-been alternative comedians, weekend messiahs, rebels with a lost cause and wannabe variety turns; Christian Cowboys in their 'Jesus loves you' embroidered zoot suits; anti-scientologists with purple alien blow-up dolls and the general air of jokey theatricality. A bunch of zealous black radicals done up like composite bouncers and bell hops with an articulate, if deluded, front man appears to be just more of the same – perfect casting.

I must have spent almost an hour in this meeting and, although it seems to be hotting up, it's also getting very repetitive and I need a change of scenery before I doze off. As I wander away and look around, those populating the scenery have changed and I now have a sense of the familiar – it's like I've just arrived. I go and pass the time of day with St Paul. I've got plenty of time and spend longer than usual doing the social rounds. I take in speakers who I've only previously experienced as hecklers. I listen to Bryan complete a spirited rant on economics. It's the first time I've heard him speak. He's another one who finishes early, before it becomes heckler-central.

It's not clever, it's not funny and I'm very tired, but when Bryan offers me his milk crate I can't refuse it and instantly decide to speak. I shouldn't have done it, but I can't resist taking advantage of what is left of the so-called civilised crowd.

I'm useless. For half an hour I struggle to keep a meeting together. When I explain that I've just got off a plane from Amsterdam and haven't slept for 24 hours, I'm heckled with "Well don't stand here boring the arse off us, go home and get some sleep." Which is as good as advice gets. I don't take it. I go and have a black coffee, shift my position and try again. This time I launch into a scheme to solve the problems surrounding race relations.

"Bad language! Bad language! Let's talk about bad language. Black and white are absolute opposites. It's probably scientifically proven. We've got to stop using black and white to describe the differences between whole swathes of humanity. Where they refer to race, both black and white must be taken out of our vocabulary."

I haven't thought this through at all, and I've got no answer to what I would replace them with, if I'd replace them at all. But it does start a lively, if fruitless, debate. Problem is, I hardly take part in it. Then someone brings me into the conversation by asking me if I heckled the Nation of Islam. This gets total focus from the crowd of twenty. I can hardly use 'being tired' as an excuse if I am also perky enough to speak. So I reply honestly.

"I never heckled or asked a question, I felt a bit intimidated and anyway I was observing."

There's groans all round. "Yeah. And? What did you think of it?"

"Well, I've always maintained that there should be a rule, that anybody who puts on a uniform must be able to administer first aid."

This gets a laugh, but I don't want it to turn trivial. I've just spent the good part of an hour listening to a man convincing me (if I didn't know already) of just how serious it all is. I'd rather say nothing than simply feed into the current clichés, but then I deliver this profundity.

"It's not a problem that excluded groups have their own agenda and exclusive membership. What becomes a problem for its members is if they are denied democratic rights within the excluded group. That is real exclusion."

After a short discussion, it's agreed by the saner members of the meeting that what is needed is that Leo Chester gets some serious feedback –

supportive heckling. Preferably from black people. All four black people present agree this is a good idea, but not one of them is up for doing it.

I lose my grip again, and very soon the meeting has deteriorated into smaller meetings. This time I don't pull it back together. Instead, I declare the area a decentralised zone and call it a day. It's now I begin to register that lots of people have got toys. I had unconsciously noticed it earlier – a little panda poking out of a pocket, a monkey sitting on a shoulder and someone playing football with a white poodle. It's only when Freemarket Kurt and his crew pass by with the free sandwiches that I see that two jokers are also distributing sentimental, soft, fluffy animals, with the worthiness of tending disaster victims.

The one problem I can report with sleeplessness is that it makes for reckless behaviour. I get a second wind and very light-headedly speak again, but this time I don't give a shit and from the start I am improvising, making mistakes and pursuing the policy of offering my harshest critics love and

understanding. I piss about with small audiences for almost another hour, and add several original bits to the oeuvre, including:

"Advertising equals desperation. Everytime you see an advert, you see desperation. If you want to know what industries are desperate, check the telly ads. Every fifteen minutes someone is desperately trying to unload something they're stuck with, you don't need, and you can't afford. Desperation! They're so desperate to sell cars. So desperate to sell computers, chat lines, insurance, television programmes, and for the last six months or so desperate to sell you a ticket for the Dome. How many people would visit the Dome if it was a word of mouth gig? 'Oooh have you heard. The government and big business have employed loads of advertising agencies to do a sort of gig in a big tent on a rubbish tip by the Thames near the Blackwall tunnel – only thirty notes'."

Finally, I stop speaking and begin to enjoy the perverse bliss that comes with fatigue. Too tired to stand, I sit on the crate propped up against the railings, experiencing the physical pleasure in yawning deeply. Someone approaches, puts a teddy bear under my arm and says "Goodnight."

Sunday 15th October 2000

Today's strategy

I now have a string of loose routines that all involve questions, answers and participation, and give me lots of opportunities for short, provocative rants, bursts of florid language, and sundry sloganeering. My strategy this week is to sustain a large crowd and consolidate this block of material which will eventually form an analysis of current society – a decoding of the zeitgeist – and inform a larky plan of action for a non-violent grassroots (and flowering tops) anarchist revolution.

The performer prepares

Paul is busy with a few people. I wave and cycle past. He calls to me and gives me a thought for the day, which I repeat under my breath and promise myself I'll remember, but promptly forget. Later I reflect again on why I forget his words so soon after hearing them. It has something to do with all the other information I take in on arrival; my anxiety and delight at being here, that gig-mode head-space about the state of the room, where to perform, who is here, all the nods and acknowledgements and various exchanges. Next week I will write it down.

I share a spliff with an old squatting comrade from the seventies. He's meeting some mates here later. They've come to support me. We wander off to heckle and browse.

Dr Stewart is surrounded by over a hundred people and is wearing big tinsel bunny ears and fancy shades. He still manages to look cool. I don't heckle, but listen. He describes every single detail and nuance he experienced on being embarrassed about farting in the tube, and even with such unpromising material, he gets so much mileage. He's not really finding any of that narrative he was after, but his delight in performing and improvising around everyday minutiae is contagious.

People's various brains! As Stewart oozes love and playful creativity while talking about farts, Soldier Dave in the neighbouring meeting is explaining with intellectual rigour – and some anger – how society can be transformed into a sharing spiritual communism. The two meetings actually converge. I push my way through and stand alongside him. Thirty faces are pointing the right way and they look very attentive. I listen, get the gist, and then make a couple of supportive interventions. On my third comment, I feel myself over-contributing and, far from supporting him, I am upsetting his flow, so I leave before it gets too disruptive.

Drug abuse and mnemonics

I gather my stuff, including my bike, which I intend to allude to, and set up under the planes. I start off with an extended version of what is becoming my opening bark.

"Bigger cages! Longer chains! Better consolation prizes!

"Bigger cages! Longer chains! Better consolation prizes!

"Wadda-we-want? Bigger cages! Longer chains! Better consolation prizes!

"All together now: Bigger cages! Longer chains! Better consolation prizes!

"Once more, with irony: Bigger cages! Longer chains! Better consolation prizes!

"Prison! We all of us live in prisons. Physical prison! Intellectual prison! Emotional prison! And Spiritual prison. This is the weekly meeting of the escape committee."

This gets a fine response, and a crowd builds up quickly. It's over fifty in a few minutes. Some people even join in the chanting, which sets the tone for a lively couple of hours. Twice, there is a sudden dwindling of numbers – once soon after I start, which I blame on my lack of joined-up thinking and lamentable short-term memory, which can only be blamed on the drugs. It registers with me that I am using mnemonics to remember even my basic material – the four varieties of prisons, for example, are assisted by the mnemonic PIES. The second crowd depletion is much later, and occurs when the Drill Sergeant initiates the Crusades in an explosion of rowdiness close by, involving the police, and virtually the whole meeting is duly distracted.

My riffs on the nature of free speech at Speakers' Corner – "free speech demands the involvement of individuals free enough to express themselves" – is beginning to convince and encourage plenty of contributions. I'm playing with it and also using it to quell the habitual pedants and spoilers, insisting they allow first-time hecklers to put their questions and points of view.

Topical dope jokes

My ex-comrades turn up in a very lively mood, and respond to my request for questions by passing me a joint and suggesting Ann Widdecombe's stance on drugs as a topic for discussion. I get a few laughs at the expense of Tim Yeo, the Tory who has again wrecked his party's efforts to launch a moral crusade. He was the first to mess up John Major's Back to Basics campaign, when it was revealed that he'd made his secretary a single-parent family. And now he is jumping on another spoiling bandwagon by admitting he's smoked dope, inhaled and enjoyed it. Like the seven other Tory front-benchers who've admitted to having a toke, it all happened when they were at university.

"What message does this send out to the youth of the country? It's alright to smoke dope if you're at university? What's that about? One law for the higher educated and one law for self-educated?"

I decide on the spot to change tack and, while flourishing a joint in one hand, I start wagging my finger in admonition at the practice.

"Well it's not alright to smoke dope! Well it's not! Just look at this bunch of middle-aged space cadets here."

I gesture to my giggling ex-comrades who are now at my side.

"They left university twenty years ago, stoned out of their tiny minds. Unemployable! Living in squats! A life of demos, festivals and parties. Then they turn up here at Hyde Park in a state of drug-crazed oblivion, probably thought there was a Stones concert on, and then they pass me the worst hash I've smoked in yonks."

Aside in a stage whisper as I return the spliff: "It's true man. It's crap dope – not suitable for speaking on, or much else. It's dozy, but not even interestingly dozy. It's strong on short-term memory loss, smells a bit stale and has little to recommend it – street wallop! And now look at me – struggling to string a sentence together."

This is the truth. The meeting suddenly gets very ragged and there's five minutes of Ann Widdecombe jokes and silly stoned banter about short-term memory loss. While some people enjoy it, many leave and the crowd halves. I drink a healthy slug of water and get a grip of the meeting, first by stopping any more joke telling from the floor, and then by telling a few of my own, calculated to improving the quality of the debate.

"Soft drugs lead on to hard drugs. I started off on cannabis and ended up on tobacco! Cigarettes – the ultimate consumer product – buy 'em, set fire to 'em and buy some more. That's 'built in obsolescence'!"

I cadge a fag, light it, and leave it smoking on the top rung of my ladder for all to see, and go on to explain that the government and the tobacco industry are not worried if you smoke or not. They honestly don't care. Just so long as you carry on buying them and paying the tax. Because you don't have to smoke them. They are quite capable of smoking themselves.

Only one person is willing to defend tobacco – Jeffrey, who has a £12 a day nicotine habit. He spends more on Marlboro in one day than I spend on dope in a week. There are a few interesting contributions about nicotine. I repeat one of them by putting Jeffrey on the spot and asking him if he agrees that "smoking a cigarette provides a brief antidote to social anxiety?" The focus is suddenly on him. He immediately lights up a ciggie and says, "No!" Perfect! How can I dislike someone who is such a perfect foil?

I have a similar growing affection for one or two other oddballs who regularly listen to me and yet disagree with just about everything I say. They are so perversely predictable.

The attendance has picked up again, and I bark to the crowds beyond to consolidate it.

"Moderation in all things! Especially moderation!"

'Im on 'is 'orse is back on duty, this time with a different horse, a white beauty, unless the dapple-grey has shed its coat in the three months since he offered me out (see 2nd July). He stops briefly as he rides pass, and when I draw attention to him he clearly doesn't want to engage and moves on immediately. I explain our relationship to the building crowd, and relate the incident in the summer, and then go on to talk about my arrests twenty years ago and throw in some fragments about Park by-laws, public hanging, and famous last words.

Plot reflection and revision

I perform these familiar anecdotes very well, with a mixture of story-telling and political sloganeering. I rarely tell them, and when I do, it's never the same way twice; they are not learned like comedy routines. The truth is, I'm not sure I could even do that now – maybe my brain is shot to shit with dope. I now realise that my plot of encouraging participation is not solely to promote democracy in the meeting – it is also one of my only modes of speaking. I now acknowledge that spontaneous storytelling is a useful adjunct too, just so long as I don't start trying to learn lots of lines – that's when the cerebral holes start appearing. So, back to the plot.

"Any questions? Come on you lazy bastards. Any questions. And don't think this has got anything to do with democracy or participation, I'm just fed up with doing all the work."

To remind them of some of the subject matter 'im on 'is 'orse rides past, covering the backs of two officers as they escort a big bruiser of a black guy out of the park.

Chairing a Debate

Now that I've slagged off the audience for not participating, I've backed myself into a bit of a corner when it comes to censuring long contributions from the floor. A fragile old lag makes a long-winded supportive statement about the police force, and then does what a lot of people do when speaking in public – unsure of where to finish, he continues speaking and ends up repeating himself in full. Disturb the comfortable, comfort the disturbed. I don't want to pull him about it, but I do want to point out the syndrome to the crowd and then, like a gift from above, a cocky young suit criticises me and does exactly the same thing, plus he jumbles his words in the realisation. I jump on him.

"Couple of points to bear in mind when you're making your contributions. For sentences, you have to get all your words in the right order – call me old-fashioned. And also make sure you stop speaking when you finished the thought, because if it's the only one you've got batting about in your head, you're gonna bore us all by repeating it; and also make sure you stop speaking when you've finished the thought, because if it's only one you've got batting about in your head, then you're gonna bore us all by repeating it. Aren't you?"

Martin browses into the meeting when it's at its largest – a hundred or so – and starts heckling. I don't listen to him. I use flattery and honesty. I tell him that he's one of the most charismatic speakers in the park and quite capable of pulling an enormous crowd of his own, so he should stop trying to poach mine. He smiles and leaves.

If I could have the perfect set-up at Speakers' Corner it would be an ensemble piece involving four or five quality control monitors in the crowd, gently heckling, constantly pulling me, keeping me on my toes, reminding me of the topical, and bringing me back on message. If I'm honest what I really want is a cross between Martin's rabid Greek chorus and Leo Chester's vigilantes. There's no reason why I can't make a public request for it, although politically I'd prefer it to evolve organically.

I'm more or less forced to take a short break when the Crusades set up next door to me. I shift position and resume the meeting on other side of the walkway.

At first only the four ex-comrades and a handful of regulars join me, so I lean on my ladder and have a chinwag. One of them, bless him, is still a squatting activist and there's a fascinating (for me) informative chat about the few remaining mass squats in London. I'm interested to learn that old established squatting communities like Oval, Grays Inn Mansions, Cromar Street, and a few others from the seventies are still there, and still locked in disputes with the local authorities. He also updates me on other properties

I remember from my days as an activist in the Ruff Tuff Creem Puff Squatters Estate Agency: Artillery Mansions, a vast nineteenth century block of flats secreted off Victoria Street opposite New Scotland Yard which has been squatted and evicted in every decade since the early seventies, is again standing empty and decaying. The mock-Goth palace that is St Pancras Station Hotel, empty for over sixty years, has been refurbished as a business centre. Huntley Street, off Tottenham Court Road, which squatters saved from dereliction in the mid-seventies and occupied for several years, only yielding when promised it would provide cheap housing for nurses, is now once again at the centre of a property dispute. There's only a dozen people listening in on this nostalgia and I decide it's time for an eviction on memory lane. I gradually start to pull a meeting together repeating aloud interesting statements, and encouraging the subject matter of current empty property, hotel space, property collateral and free market housing.

In the middle of this, a newcomer asks what we are talking about. I explain "You know how you have to sweat your bollocks off working just so you can pay rent or a mortgage? And how your landlord hardly spends anything on maintenance or suchlike? Well, we were discussing where your money went. Whether it went into buying more property so he could rip off more people, or whether it was gambled on the money market casinos. Where is it? The money you work so hard for? Is it in some tax-haven bank in the Cayman Islands or sloshing around in some dodgy hedge fund in the city."

I finally guide the text round to my familiar topical rant on 'Don't protest about petrol prices! Go protest about rents, mortgages and land ownership!' This attracts a crowd of fifty plus, although the numbers seem to fluctuate wildly today, varying from twenty to a hundred in a matter of minutes.

Critical Mass

Before the comrades leave they hand me a leaflet, which I'm happy to read out. It announces the next Critical Mass demo – the regular protest by hundreds of cyclists that takes place on the last Friday of every month, starting 6pm at the Embankment, and taking a chaotic route around central London disrupting and bringing traffic to a standstill in its wake. A startling looking, middle-aged, femme fatale straight out of a Hammer movie – never seen her before, never seen her since – proclaims on leaving "I won't be able to attend; I no longer have a monthly cycle." Everyone's a comedian, but they are rarely as witty as that.

An elegant explanation of the theory of critical mass comes from someone who I've always considered one of the terminally mad. I am so knocked out by his contribution that I pause and quietly beat myself up about under estimating him in the past. He, meanwhile, responds to those around him who want to hear more, ignores me, and starts talking to them. It quickly escalates into an alternative meeting. I then get very shirty, interrupt, and explain:

"For the last two years, up until five minutes ago, he's been silent and suddenly he's an elegant heckler and then he's a fledgling speaker and now, I'm going to have to kick him out of the nest. Oi! Outta here! Go and start your own meeting."

He leaves but is back in a few minutes, a bit sheepish. From here, I move on to applying the motif of Critical Mass to building an alternative infrastructure for the new peasants' revolution, based on setting up self-sufficient communities and autonomous zones throughout the UK, until the point of critical mass when the dominant economic culture collapses and is usurped by the ascendant anarcho-utopian paradise. Yeah, crazy! Mail me the forms! I open it out to the meeting

"Let's start a revolution. All in the name of art, of course. I feel a political organisation coming on. Federation of Landless Organised Peasants. FLOP! Perfect! It's got everything; even Post-mod up-its-own-arse irony."

Within five minutes the revolution has modified its demands to an ironic slogan.

"Don't give money to the homeless they'll only spend it on drugs. Don't give money to landlords they'll only spend it on far more expensive drugs."

Male egos at five paces

Arch spoiler The Appalling Lurch oozes the relentless confidence that comes from being born into privilege; he's apparently extraordinarily thick-

Tony Allen auctioning a plane tree

skinned, and oblivious to criticism. On his occasional visits to the park, he spends a fair bit of time heckling in my meeting. I'm only mildly flattered. I don't like him, and I'm sure the feeling's mutual. I'm not sure whether I'm winning these sporadic slanging matches, but he's certainly losing. Nevertheless, he inevitably disrupts what I'm saying, and I'm forced to duel with him on his own nitpicky, public school boy, smartarse level.

He often arrives with his own audience, who follow him around swelling the size of the meetings he visits. The laughter from his early sniping inevitably attracts more. In fact, the advocate heckler role of my original one thousand artists project is based on the traditional peripatetic hecklers of which the towering Lurch is the latest exponent. I understand the terrain and I'm always ready for him.

"There were twenty people in this meeting before you arrived and now there are sixty. What can we deduce from that? Twenty people want to listen to me. And forty people want to listen to you … being humiliated by me. Male egos at five paces – my favourite. This man is a masochist. That's why he comes to my meeting, because he wants a verbal beating. Cos he's a maso. Aren't you? Look at him. He'd love me to metaphorically cut him down to size! Go away. I'm not doing it. Unless you pay me."

I have one-upped him, and he is quiet. A minute later he rallies and, as soon as he gets a laugh at my expense, he does something I haven't seen him do before – he calls a truce and lets me speak unhindered. I can feel the unease in his system as he yields to me. This is a new tactic. How much space is he prepared to give me?

An old lag with a heavily stained waistcoat heckles me with something I don't hear and which nobody laughs at. Lurch deals with him.

"Is that your dinner jacket? Because it's got your dinner all down the front of it!"

Heckling my hecklers is an act of support. He's offering me an oily hand of allegiance.

How squatting saved Victorian London
I get politically provocative to see how far I can push it. "Squatting saved Victorian London" I announce. He scoffs, and then bids me continue.

"Government Housing policy of the late sixties was to knock down the crumbling grandeur of London's inner city Victorian terraces and replace them with tower blocks and housing estates. They placed CPOs – Compulsory Purchase Orders – on the old property and then spent years moving the tenants around and gradually trashing and tinning up the voids. The remaining tenants didn't like living in an urban wilderness, and they quickly became sympathetic to the presence of squatters. It wasn't unknown for tenants moving out to give their keys to squatters groups. Houses were quickly occupied as soon as they became available. When the demolition teams arrived to knock them down to make way for the next tower block, they were confronted with organised residents groups of squatters and non-eligible council tenants. North Paddington and North Kensington, where I was living, was almost entirely Victorian residential.

"Was that here in London?" asks an American tourist with his arm around his partner, who is fiddling with her camera. My new bouncer scoffs at them and gets a laugh.

"The rest of Kensington was also Victorian residential but they weren't about to knock that down and build tower blocks. Because that's where Lurch and all the high Tories and half the government lived and still live.

"Over the next few years they changed their minds about tower blocks. This was partly because it was a stupid idea in the first place and partly because of 'the economy, stupid', they could no longer afford to do it. Which meant great tracts of London were a building site with large squatting communities occupying the neighbouring condemned housing.

"In 1975, I was part of an anarchist network organising the squatting of empty property throughout the capital under the slogan 'Squat now while stocks last' and 'Pull down the tin and let the people in!' In Westminster that year we housed more people than the local Westminster council housing department.

"By 1977, one report said that in London alone there was 100,000 squatters plus another 100,000 of legitimised squatters living in short-life housing.

"By 1979 the policy was finally changed. 'Renovate the Victorian terraces and divide and rule the squatters.' The more articulate and organised of the squatters did a range of deals with the various councils and ended up living as co-ops or as council tenants on controlled rents in the renovated Victorian terraces. It may not have been a deliberate anarchist policy, but nevertheless the squatters of the seventies saved Victorian London.

"That's why I've got a nice cheap flat in Ladbroke Grove."

I now turn on Lurch.

"And that's why I hate you. Because 25 years later, you and your property speculator ilk are playing monopoly with my gift to the nation."

"Ah" is his top comment. No heckle. No argument. Except an oily courtesy, which I don't trust.

"Righto! Here's one ..." he says

Puns, wit and slapstick.

Now he expects me to allow him to make an unhindered contribution. He keeps it short. The closest he can come to an on-message joke about squatting and housing is the hoary old chestnut "Why does Karl Marx drink herbal tea?"

Anarchists in particular are bored with this crap pun, and there's enough of them present to muster a chorus of groans before he's even got to the punchline.

"Because proper tea is theft."

Hardly anyone laughs but the groans increase. This gives me the cue to go into teacher mode. I'm shaking my head and looking very disappointed with him.

"Not only is it a crap joke, it's an old crap joke and what's more the original quotation is not Karl Marx, it is the anarchist philosopher Pierre-Joseph Proudhon – 'Property is Theft, Property is Liberty, Property is Impossible'. An elegant and witty paradox that resonates its subject matter. Unlike the crap pun that your joke depended on. Puns are the joke form of the intellectually arrested. Do you still read the Dandy and Beano? A pun is a form of word play that unites two things that have no reason to be united, other than the rather dull fact that their names sound similar. 'Proper tea is a genuine beverage,' enough information. Wit however, which in your case you have not got, is a form of word-play that unites two things or ideas and suggests lateral comparisons, forcing us to re-consider our understanding of one, other or both of them. Wit enlightens us, enriches us."

Lurch has been trying to interrupt, but he bites his tongue and, when I've finished and received a 'wooe' from some of the regulars for being such a clever bastard, he continues his policy of bonhomie. It's horribly false but he's on the back foot. Is this the way he deals with his betters and unknown quantities? He's joshing with me, the toady. Now he wants to redeem himself and tell another joke. He's hardly heckled me for five, maybe ten, minutes and he wants a reward.

"It's a joke about MI5 and I promise it will be good" he ingrates.

Some of the crowd don't have my insight or knowledge of him, and he has enough tacit support for me to feel churlish if I don't give him the space. It's a long one. Of course it is. I regret it immediately. I've got myself into this. It's nearly the end of the day. So let's make it difficult for myself. I contemplate plan B. Play it by ear and think laterally. Don't heckle, don't even listen to the joke, but don't let him finish it.

Plan B better be good. I love doing this to myself; every now and again I hit gold.

Lurch embarks on telling his joke, dealing with a few minor heckles along the way. Some people leave. They didn't come here to listen to an upper-class buffoon tell jokes in an anarchist meeting. No sense of the ludicrous, some people. There's still about fifty paying attention. Some are hardened Hyde Park regulars who are well aware that Lurch and I are old adversaries. They've been in the meeting long enough to know that the situation is unusual. Others know nothing because they've only been in the meeting for five minutes, check, they've only been in the country for five hours.

I'm not listening to him. I'm observing the crowd. I notice that many of them keep looking back at me to check how I'm receiving the joke-telling. That's all I need. I inhabit my clown – Tofu the Zany, a mute alter ego who is a cross between Good Soldier Svejk and Harpo Marx.

"So the second candidate, the Russian …" Lurch continues "… comes in and they ask him the same question. What …"

Less than sixty seconds in, and I've got it. He won't get to the third candidate and the punchline. All I have to do is yawn, close my eyes, and pretend to fall asleep out of sheer boredom. Then draw attention to myself by snoring very loudly, and spectacularly fall off the ladder and bring it clattering down on top of me, wake up and say, "Has he finished?" It's beautiful. It's simple, and I manage to screw it up big time.

First rule of comedy.

There are some spontaneous stunts and pratfalls that have to be executed with impeccable timing and to witness them is to be privileged. To have them occur to you and then to perform them is an experience better than the experience that was said to be better than sex. This was a full breath away from such an experience. I yawn theatrically. I close my eyes. I wait for a pause and … and I fail to snore. I don't snore! For some reason I miss-snore, I get a kick, whatever! First rule of comedy – timing. I try again but by then I'm snoring as I clatter to the ground and no one hears it. Some people laugh, some people have been watching me, but most of them need an explanation. Some people think I've hurt myself and have come to my aid

"Has he finished?" I say, "I fell asleep." Another laugh, but it's only a tenth of the hoot it could have been if I'd got that snore on cue. I am inwardly beating myself up at the lost opportunity. I console myself 'There is always another time'. But 'first time' is the prize.

Lurch is now trying to focus attention to complete his joke. I'm having none of it.

"Well I'm not listening to your sodding joke." I scream with displaced anger. "I never wanted to hear it in the first place."

Ladder in hand, I stomp off and move the meeting ten yards away with half the audience filtering after me.

"Thirty years an artist and an anarchist and it's come to this!" I declare. "Reduced to doing an unsuccessful double act with The Appalling Lurch for American tourists at Speakers' Corner."

"Yeah, and on an Arts Council grant" quips a voice just below me.

"Nice one Albert. Thank you."

HOW I BECAME A PROFESSIONAL HECKLER

March 2000. I start the new millennium as I intend to continue – with a little help from my friends, I have spent the evening attempting to fill in an application form for Arts Council funding. We fail miserably. It is beyond us – we don't speak the language, and now we've started on the wine which we brought along to celebrate the completion of the job. Questions are being read aloud and the jargon ridiculed; wacky and unlikely art projects are being described; we are giggling like kids and snarling like thwarted adults. The forms are being scribbled on, screwed up and thrown around the room. Then, amidst all the daft comments and lateral behaviour, a way forward presents itself ...

Year of the Artist – Application text (1)

I propose to go on a short speaking tour of Great Britain presenting ideas and chairing debates on the subject of Funding the Socially Excluded Artist in the Year 2000 and Beyond.

As part of my presentation, I will read out a selection of the most interesting and imaginative unsubmitted proposals from artists excluded from the Year of the Artist scheme because they couldn't meet the assessment criteria, were intimidated and/or infuriated by the paperwork and involvement with the arts bureaucracy, or had resolved never to sit another examination again and consequently excluded themselves.

I also wish to give voice to an increasingly coherent set of ideas that argues for the state benefit system to acknowledge its unwitting role as initial funder of the isolated artist and grassroots group, and change its policy from niggardly persecution to constructive support.

Throughout the tour I intend to invite a cross-section of guest speakers selected not only for their challenging and imaginative ideas, their performance and public speaking skills, but because they represent artists from, or working in, culturally and socially excluded communities.

The host groups will consequently reflect this background and the venues for the event will be at the grass roots of community arts, i.e. musicians' collectives, unemployed centres, community colleges, pub function rooms, free festival tents and short-life occupations / squats.

Essential to the artistic integrity of each event is an after-gig party and cabaret, presenting an opportunity to showcase local talent. This will be organised by the host group with assistance from the project managers (New Agenda Arts Trust).

I was inspired to submit this project because it combines both my current artistic style – which is a crossover MC / standup comedian / public speaker – with content which has, in my five years as artistic director and co-administrator of a small arts charity, become close to an obsession.

I was also inspired to submit this proposal because whenever I broach the subject in a public arena, and express my frustration, there is always a section of the audience who howl approval.

Further inspiration came from my introduction to a literary sub-genre of spoof project ideas and, if the rules didn't restrict me to one idea, I would submit the following as my second string.

I propose to graffiti motor way bridges, advertising hoardings, and appropriate government buildings with the legend 'HONK IF YOU'RE A SOCIALLY EXCLUDED ARTIST'. I am however willing to amend the text to 'HONK IF YOU'RE A SOCIALLY INCLUDED ARTIST' should my proposal be accepted.

• The quality of the artistic content planned

In recent years I have been running regular stand up comedy and performance workshops, experimenting with an ensemble, and developing my own solo show into something that starts off traditionally enough as stand-up comedy but which inevitably finds me in the role of chairing a brainstorming session. I have been learning how to control these situations: how to censure, how to encourage, how to appear hands-off while maintaining responsibility for the attention of the entire audience. For the last eighteen months I have been proving to myself that what I am involved in is still an art form; especially when one wag described my gig as "an anarchists' Jerry Springer show without the all-in wrestling". As a consequence I deliberately took on a number of non-artistic roles, including attending and then chairing a regular campaign meeting of a hundred participants, to help me clarify and understand the expectations of an audience member at an arts event as opposed to a participant in a political meeting. Having said that, there are meetings and meetings – my return, after several years, to a regular slot at Speaker's Corner only reminded me of that venue's unique dynamics and potential for artistic expression.

- **The potential to increase awareness of the positive role of the artist in society**

To broach taboos, kick the stuff about and present a shared truth to the tribe was traditionally the role of the shaman. In the year two thousand, the information revolution and globalisation is fast-forwarding human affairs into a reductionist virtual monoculture and, conversely by default, a cultural Babel of virtual communities for the alienated and the isolated. Live intimate performance has the unique potential for authentic communion.

I believe that it is the duty of the contemporary artist to sort the time and place and rise to the occasion.

- **The degree to which the residency extends creative opportunities for artists**

Following the annual trek of thousands of other socially excluded artists, I intend to do research literally in the field – on the Summer Festival circuit – starting with the speakers' tent in the Green Futures field at Glastonbury in the second week of June and finishing with the Exodus dance party at Long Meadow Farm, Luton, on August bank holiday.

It is familiar, if unfirm, territory but invariably helps me shape up my performance skills and ideas in front of a variety of unconventional and challenging audiences, as well as bringing me into contact with artists from a myriad of disciplines.

I propose to start the tour proper at the end of September and stage the event in twelve locations across the country over a six-week period.

• The potential for excellence in the planning and organisation of the residency
New Agenda Arts Trust will manage the project by way of a partnership supplying a part-time administrator and will cover office and advertising costs.

An established internet consultancy have agreed to sponsor the online presence and to supply a domain name, advertise the events, publish related text and project documentation, design the site and offer guidance with the selection of web assets.

An online campaign organisation have agreed to sponsor by way of supplying a customised email data base with reliable conduits to the projects offline target groups.

• How will you ensure equality of opportunity throughout your project?
I am currently negotiating to broadcast each event as a multi-media remixed message millennium extravaganza live on the internet using equipment fuelled by pedal power and manned by wealthy, white, sane, able-bodied, higher-educated, heterosexual, male thirtysomethings.

Tony Allen
April 2000

The Year of the Artist people replied and were surprisingly affirming. They invite me in for a chat where it is made quite clear that, although they like my critique of arts funding, they are not in the business of picking up the tab for me and my mates to hold a series of parties up and down the country. Although this is a clear knockback, I am informed they would still consider a London specific project. "The London YOTA deadline being in ten days time, perhaps you should consider a simple solo application."

So it is a positive response after all. I have to make my mind up pretty quick. What am I doing that can be described as art, and that I can carry on doing without breaking my stride?

Year of the Artist – Application text (2)

I propose to be an advocate heckler at Speaker's Corner and challenge the dominant and traditional mode of presenting ideas. My residency will be the culmination of a process 25 years in the realisation.

My residency will add an element of playful honesty to the proceedings at Speaker's Corner where the current mode is confrontation and reductionist humour. This will benefit the thousands of weekly visitors, the hundreds of regulars and twenty to thirty or so regular speakers.

I intend to do more research during the summer months and then start the residency proper on the first Sunday of September, then every following Sunday for six weeks.

My partners for the project will be an established (four years) internet design outfit who will document the proceedings; and a registered (1995) arts charity dedicated to supporting innovative performance who will manage and promote the project.

Both of these partners have been approached and have agreed to sponsor/partner the residency.

• The quality of the artistic content planned

My experience of speaking on sexual politics at Hyde Park in the seventies gave me a wealth of material for my stand up comedy act with Alternative Cabaret and at the Comedy Store in 1979. During my career as a performer, I have kept in touch with Speakers Corner and over the years have taken the opportunity to work out ideas for solo shows from the third rung of a step-ladder to motley crowds on a Sunday afternoon in the Park. In the nineties, I started running regular workshops in stand up comedy and as a consequence began deconstructing the art of the performer. My research has led me to consider other performance disciplines and cross-overs. It has convinced me of the unique status of what happens at Speaker's Corner and its great potential for artistic expression.

• The potential to increase awareness of the positive role of the artist in society

The project will involve spells of speaking when, as well as explaining my artistic mission, filling in on the local history and answering questions, I will also offer to put questions to other speakers on behalf of audience members who have found the bigger, rowdier meetings too intimidating to speak up for themselves. I will consequently spend some of my time in an advocacy role, taking my audience on a guided tour of the other speakers and interrupting them when appropriate.

• The degree to which the residency extends creative opportunities for artists
In my most recent visits to the Park, I have experimented with both speaking and heckling, style and content, and applying the action motto 'Comfort the disturbed, disturb the comfortable'. Sympathising with the pain of raging bigots and the embarrassment of insulted tourists led to a variety of delightful and creative exchanges.

There are precedents for this sort of peripatetic role and most of them have been unwelcome. Most notoriously was the rabble-rousing heckler and reactionary Lord Barker in the late seventies, who was often to be seen followed around by a huge crowd of thrill-seekers. Also, there has been the occasional phenomenon over the years of the Heckler's Union, a fairly arbitrary group comprised of frustrated speakers and sundry spoilers. Similarly, their antics have never been applauded by the majority of regulars. I believe that I am developing a style of heckling which undermines the traditional reductionist banter, but more importantly, is not seen by other speakers as a disruptive activity.

• The potential for excellence in the planning and organisation of the residency
I will co-manage the project with a small team under the sponsorship of New Agenda Arts Trust who I have been associated with for many years, running the Performance Club, and organising concerts and cabaret events.

NAAT have agreed to supply a part-time administrator and cover office and advertising costs.

An established internet consultancy have agreed to sponsor the on-line presence and to supply a domain name, advertise the event, publish related text, design the site and offer guidance with the selection of web assets.

• How will you ensure equality of opportunity throughout your project?
I will ensure equality of opportunity throughout the project by not excluding

participants by confronting them with impenetrable forms, confusing them with complicated jargon or by subjecting them to unnecessary procedures. Neither will I enforce a strict assessment criteria for participation.

All of the above I believe favours the higher educated and insults the already socially excluded.

And they went for it.

Further Reading

Attitude! Wanna make something of it? by Tony Allen (Gothic Image, 2003)

Hyde Park Orator by Bonar Thompson (Jarrolds, 1936)

The Speakers by Heathcote Williams (Calder & Boyars, 1974)

Stilled Tongues by Stephen Coleman (Porcupine Press, 1997)

Speakers' Corner: an illustrated anthology edited by Jim Huggon (Kropotkin's Lighthouse Publications, 1977)

Websites

http://www.newagenda.demon.co.uk/

http://www.speakerscorner.net/

http://www.anyoldicon.com

Radio

Resonancefm.com

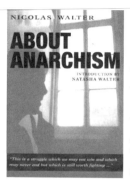

ABOUT ANARCHISM
by Nicolas Walter
introduction by Natasha Walter

This is a new edition of the classic work by Nicolas Walter, who was a writer, journalist and active protester against the power of the state. It has often been reprinted and been translated into many languages, including French, Spanish, Japanese, Serbo-Croat, Chinese, Polish and Russian. It includes a new introduction by Natasha Walter.

£4.20 (including postage and packing)   *ISBN 0 900384 90 5*

ANARCHY IN ACTION
by Colin Ward

This book is not intended for people who have spent a lifetime pondering the problems of anarchism, but for those who either had no idea of what the word implied or knew exactly what it implied and rejected it, considering that it had no relevance for the modern world. It is about the many ways in which people organise themselves in any kind of human society ...

£5.95 (including postage and packing)   *ISBN 0 900384 20 4*

WHAT IS ANARCHISM?
An Introduction

Today the word anarchism inspires both fear and fascination, but few people seem to understand what anarchists believe, what anarchists want and what anarchists do. To help answer these questions are contributions from Michael Bakunin, Alexander Berkman, William Godwin, Peter Kropotkin, Errico Malatesta, William Morris, Rudolf Rocker, Donald Rooum, Philip Sansom, Colin Ward and many others.

£3.50 (including postage and packing)   *ISBN 0 900384 66 2*

Our full booklist is available from Freedom Press,
84b Whitechapel High Street, London E1 7QX or see our website at
www.freedompress.org.uk

WHY WORK?
Arguments for the Leisure Society

Here the distinction is made between work and employment, between useful work and useless toil. This book includes contributions from Bertrand Russell, William Morris, Clifford Harper, Colin Ward and many others. "No working ideal for machine production can be based solely on the gospel of work … we must examine in detail the processes that lead up to the final state of leisure, free activity, freedom."

£5.95 *(including postage and packing)*   ISBN 0 900384 25 5

GEORGE ORWELL AT HOME
and Among the Anarchists

Here for the first time is a full collection of the photographs by Vernon Richards showing George Orwell both at home and in unexpectedly informal settings, and which give an unusually intimate view of an extremely private man. These photographs are accompanied by a series of essays on George Orwell from the anarchist perspective by Vernon Richards, Colin Ward and Nicolas Walter.

£8.50 *(including postage and packing)*   ISBN 0 900384 94 8

WILLIAM BLAKE
by Peter Marshall

William Blake was a poet, painter, engraver and visionary. Considered eccentric, if not mad, in his own time, he now appears as a key figure in English romanticism. This study offers a lively and perceptive account of Blake's thought and presents him as a forerunner of modern anarchism and social ecology, and reveals the light which shines behind the misty mountain range of Blake's symbolism and mythology.

£4.50 *(including postage and packing)*   ISBN 0 900384 77 8

All available from Freedom Press, 84b Whitechapel High Street, London E1 7QX (payment with order please) or via our website at www.freedompress.org.uk

Freedom Press also publishes the anarchist
paper *Freedom*. For our current subscription
rates contact us at: Freedom Press,
84b Whitechapel High Street, London E1 7QX
or visit our website at
www.freedompress.org.uk